## ABOUT THE AUTHORS

Margaret and Erling Wold combine personal and professional insights in this popular book. Their marriage is a living model of Christian love and service, and they draw on knowledge gained as active leaders in the Marriage Encounter movement. While pastor of a large congregation in Garden Grove, California, Erling counseled many couples. They are now members of the faculty at California Lutheran University in Thousand Oaks, where they teach theology courses and counsel students.

Margaret and Erling Wold are coauthors of several books, the most recent, *Great God of Love*. Margaret is also the author of *The Shalom Woman*, *Women of Faith and Spirit*, and *The Power of Ordinary Christians*.

# Bible Readings
# FOR
# COUPLES

# Bible Readings
## FOR COUPLES

## Margaret & Erling Wold

**AUGSBURG** Publishing House • Minneapolis

## PREFACE

Dear Loving Couple,

How do we go about selecting 100 Bible readings from the possible thousands which have a word for couples?

Faced with that dilemma, we decided to start with the one that sets the tone for our relationship, two verses from the Song of Solomon.

Then, because we believe every book of the Bible is rich with meaning for all of us, we have chosen at least one passage from each of the 66 books. They appear in biblical order, so if you read five of these pages a week, you will touch every book of the Bible in five months.

The next time around you may discover other verses in each book besides those we selected. But the ones we have chosen represent the whole of our own theory and practice of commitment and love.

Our own love as a couple has deepened in the sharing of these words; may yours deepen as you read them. Above all, may Jesus Christ become more real as the third person in your relationship, creating a holy triangle of love!

Margaret and Erling Wold

# ■ DEAREST, I LOVE YOU (OVER) . . .

Song of Sol. 8:6-7: "Love is as powerful as death" (v. 6).

For one year of our life different assignments forced us to live two thousand miles apart. That space made touching impossible and telephone calls unsatisfying.

We began to value written words in a new way. Letters could be read over and over again. Tucked away in pocket or purse, they became extensions of the other person available for touching and holding.

One letter sent by Erling to me was only ten words long and looked like this:

| *front side* | *back side* |
|---|---|
| Dearest, | Dearest, |
|    I |    I |
|       love |       love |
|          you. |          you. |
|   ( over ) |   ( over ) |

"Love is as powerful as death. . . ." Over and over again I turned that single sheet of paper. Love is eternal; it never ends. I carried that letter wherever I went and it became a seal upon my heart.

God, you are everlasting love. Motivate us to create our love in the image of yours.

**Write a love letter to your mate. Exchange them.**

# ■ DESIGNED TO BE CREATIVE

Gen. 1:27-28: "He created them male and female" (v. 27).

We share an exciting beginning. Made in God's image, we are brothers and sisters before we are lovers and mates. Our validity and value are born from this eternal relationship, making us sensitive to vast dreams, large horizons, creative impulses.

In Genesis we see two persons, a woman and a man, both reflections of God's being and purposes, prototypes of every other man and woman who have ever walked the long corridors of history.

Be productive and nurturing, God tells us. Let life flow on through you. Create!—children, families, crops, herds, goods, services, art forms, music, and communities.

The whole world waits for our tender, loving care. "Man and woman, care for my earth," God commands. We are to polish the earth, enrich it, and handle it with care.

God created us and everything else good. Our job? To keep on reproducing God's image in everything we do, and nurture God's good earth.

Creating God, we hear your challenge to live creative and nurturing lives. Help us to mark our world with your image.

**List ways you are living in a productive and nurturing relationship.**

# ■ TOGETHER IS GOOD

Gen. 2:18:  "It is not good for the man to live alone."

Only about five percent of the people in the United States stay single all their lives. Sixty percent of first marriages last until death comes for one of the partners.

The longing to be mated runs deep in most people, and the "boy-meets-girl-meets-boy" theme dominates our literature. Many singles who are happy in their careers and enjoy solitary pursuits still confess that their aloneness is often unbearable.

Loneliness haunts all of us—married or single, woman or man, young or old, rich or poor. Only the Spirit of God can touch and fill that certain lonely God-shaped void in each one's spirit.

But next-best is to find someone who seems specially created to be one's own mate, one's own "helper." The Hebrew word for "helper" is *ezer*, and it's used 21 times in the Old Testament. Sixteen of these times *ezer* refers to God as our helper—energizing, renewing, and rescuing.

Isn't that what we all long for in a mate? Someone who picks us up when we're down; someone we can renew when he or she is down. Lonely humans long for someone who will dispel their aloneness.

God heard our cry, even before we knew it was there, and gave us each other. We are together. We are no longer alone.

Helping God, help us to be *ezer* to each other.

**Do you tell each other when you need help? If you don't, how can your mate know and respond? Share clues to your moods.**

11

# ■ THE CLOSER, THE BETTER

Gen. 2:24: ". . . and they become one."

We're finally married. It was a long time happening. I met you such a long time before we got together. Or so it seemed.

It was love at first sight with me. I remember so vividly falling into your eyes, tumbling end over end into their depths. Now my dreams are consummated.

"Be close," says God. "Be closer to one another than to anyone else in the whole world." I have to practice this daily, leaving parents, job, children, and hobbies. To give my mate top priority demands more than I am by nature willing to give. But the closeness we feel when I do is worth the effort. I'm glad God created us to be one flesh.

Closeness means opening up to you, letting you in on my hidden self, making myself vulnerable to you. Sometimes I'm afraid you might think me dumb, foolish, or evil when I reveal myself, but that's the risk I have to take to insure continuing closeness. I try to trust you that much.

And it means that I will "pleasure" you. No other physical delight can touch making love. The touching, the caressing, the ecstasy all add to the richness of "cleaving" to each other.

Hold us close, Jesus, that we may choose to be close to each other.

**What are the obstacles to closeness in your relationship? How can you practice closeness?**

# ■ SIN'S TERRIBLE FALLOUT

Gen. 3:16-19: "You were made from soil, and you will become soil again" (v. 19).

Death. It will separate us some day. I can hardly bear the thought. Never to touch you again. Never to hold you close. Never to exchange words or to laugh over private jokes. Never again to meet your eyes across the room and feel the spark of love glow in my spirit.

Death already casts its shadow over our relationship. Ugly words pass between us—unwanted and regretted, but there. Resentments and angers flare and tempers boil over. We compete for first place and deal in subtle rivalries. We hurt one another, knowing exactly where the other can most easily be "killed."

In our dyings comes the promise of God. The offspring of the woman will crush the snake's head (Gen. 3:15). He does, he does! Jesus is here! Into all of our angers and pains, our struggles and hurts, he comes with healing.

I love you, dearest. I don't want to wound you. Let's not be in bondage to death anymore.

Let's not let it separate us *now*.

Jesus of the realized promise, help us live beyond the fallout of sin.

Identify and write down marks of death in your relationship. Tear up or burn the paper and bury it. Let it become ashes and soil.

# ■ GOD MAKES LAUGHTER THE GLUE OF LOVE

Gen. 17:17; 18:12: "Abraham . . . began to laugh. . . . Sarah laughed."

Every morning something tickles our joy into laughter. We have discovered how healing, blending, and therapeutic laughter proves to be in our relationship.

Sarah and Abraham discovered that God is the one who makes laughter for us (Gen. 21:6). Right in the face of their cynicism and rebellion, he created laughter. How funny that an old man and an old woman should have sexual pleasure and produce a baby! What an incongruity! But God did it! And the baby, God said, was to be named Isaac, which means "laughter."

Laughter is the glue that holds love together when it could fall into a thousand pieces. It preserves relationships in tough moments. Humor puts tyrants in perspective and keeps the oppressed sane. Battlefield surgeons find that laughter makes the horror of their task bearable.

We have our private "couple" jokes. They're ours alone, reminders of past moments shared, secrets kept. Sometimes they bubble up in the strangest moments and give a lilt to life again.

Whenever Sarah and Abraham looked into the baby face of their miracle child Laughter, they saw the face of the God who keeps doing the impossible and the incongruous. And we can all laugh again.

God of all joy, cement our love with shared laughter.

**What private, funny happenings and secrets do you share? Remind each other of them often. They are your laughter-glue from God.**

# ■ ENGRAVE ME ON YOUR HEART

Gen. 29:20: "seven years . . . seemed like only a few days to him."

Can you believe Jacob? Are there really people like that? A man who falls so madly in love that he's willing to wait and work seven years for a woman, and another seven to complete the bargain?

That's hard to believe, but apparently a first meeting can etch a face so deeply and permanently on a person's heart that no rival can ever replace it. An outsider may say, "I wonder what he sees in her," or "How can she be so wrapped up in him?" But the lover sees only the beauty in the beloved.

Jacob's love was always for Rachel only. Even when her father cruelly deceived him by substituting his older daughter in the marriage ceremony, Jacob accepted it as a small price for his incomparable love. Fourteen years of labor and responsibility for an unwanted second wife and her children were nothing compared to finally winning Rachel!

If Jacob were one of today's shutterbugs, his camera would no doubt be focused constantly on Rachel. Friends would probably be subjected to endless showings of her picture. Long after her beauty faded for others, Jacob would see her through the picture engraved on his heart. And for him the years that passed would always, like that original seven, seem but a few days.

 Lord, give us eyes only for each other.

**Carry a picture of your mate wherever you go. Look at it frequently.**

# ■ A SPOONFUL OF SUGAR

Exod. 20:2-3: ". . . out of Egypt, where you were slaves" (v. 2).

Her husband wanted to leave her for a couple of months to live with a bachelor friend, the young wife said, just to see "how it felt to be free again."

Those tantalizing thoughts *do* tempt partners occasionally. Oh, to be irresponsible and unrestrained once more! No duties, no obligations, no restrictions on personal freedom! Laws, rules, responsibilities—who needs them?

Growing up, that process toward adulthood which focuses the dreams of every child, brings responsibility. Reality may seem less than the dream. Like the young husband, one can run from responsibility. Wives and husbands can be persuaded to let go, the law can be evaded, people who trust and rely on us can be hoodwinked.

But ultimately we face God himself. And we face his immutable, unchangeable, and unarguable commandments. The only way to get around the law is to deny the Lawgiver.

Strong medicine, God's law. But God's no springs out of the love of the one who brought you ". . . out of Egypt, where you were slaves." God's love and grace sweeten the sting of his law and make it the seedbed of a productive relationship.

Help us to meditate on your law, Lord, so that we may love it and accept it as your gracious gift.

**Have you ever wanted to escape the responsibilities of marriage? How did you sweeten duty for each other?**

# ■ MAKING UP

Lev. 16:34: ". . . once a year . . . to purify the people."

Wouldn't it be great to have one day a year set aside for wiping the slate clean? Every unkind word, every adulterous thought, every mean action—gone! God provided a day like that for the people of Israel, the day of atonement, a meaningful time to confess and make amends.

Whenever joy vanishes from a relationship and shadows darken love's sunshine, festering sins may be the cause. Couples can set aside a specific time for hearing confessions and granting pardon. The sacrifice would not be bulls or goats but the sacrifice of a humble and repentant heart (Ps. 51:17). "I'm sorry, darling, forgive me."

Love *does* mean saying you're sorry and being forgiven. We don't demand reparations for wrongs committed against us by those we love, but in our wisdom we allow them to make amends if *they* need to do that. The act of sacrifice gave the ritual of atonement its meaning. The act of Christ's crucifixion makes God's love for us real. An act of love toward the one sinned against helps us "make up."

Lord, help us clear the air between us through our words and deeds.

**Think of some task your beloved hates to do. Offer to do it as an act of love.**

# ■ SOMEONE TO COME HOME TO

Num. 35:9-15:   "These will serve as cities of refuge" (v. 15).

All through the day, out there "doing my thing," I'm looking forward to coming home to my beloved. If I'm feeling like a failure, if I'm tired, if I've goofed and unintentionally hurt someone, I know that when I come home I'll find my beloved there. We'll hold each other, listen to each other's stories, confess our failures, and find comfort.

God told the people of Israel to set up "cities of refuge" where those who had unintentionally killed someone would be safe from avengers. The law of "an eye for an eye" could not be exacted there.

Where will we find such a refuge in our world if we don't find it with our mate? We know perfectly well we are not blameless. Our frailties get us in trouble so often. When we come home battle-scarred from arenas where "an eye for an eye" is the vicious law, we need to be soothed with the oil of love and revived with the wine of forgiveness.

Even if one of us has intentionally brought pain to someone else, the other can point the way to the source of grace and forgiveness, Jesus our Lord. Hand in hand we can run to him for refuge.

Lord, help us make our home a place of refuge for each other.

**Set aside some time each day for listening to and comforting each other. Share with your mate what form of comforting helps you most.**

# ■ WHERE LOVE BEGINS

Deut. 6:4-9: "Love the Lord your God with all your heart . . ." (v. 5).

Do you have a car you love so much that you wax it every week? Or plants you care for so tenderly that you almost cry over every wilting leaf? And yet we often tell each other, "I love you more than anything else in the whole world!"

Does loving God with all our heart, soul, and strength mean we can't passionately love anything else? God doesn't say that. In fact, just the opposite is true. If you commit yourself to loving God with all the passion of your being, you will be more inclined to love yourself and others and to care for your possessions.

Everything falls into its proper place when God comes first. A personalized license plate might read "OILUVZ" to proclaim the owner's love for a "Z." Our houses are lovingly decorated. But cars and houses can be sold and replaced.

The *shema* (Deut. 6:4-9) was recited twice a day in every Israelite home as a reminder that the Lord was never to be replaced in that house. Only the Spirit of God dwelling within us can make us love God completely. But if you want your love for each other to be permanent, you will start by passionately loving God.

Lord God, let our love for each other spring out of our passion for you.

**Create your own personal *shema* of love and recite it together each day.**

# ■ HAVING FUN

Deut. 24:5: ". . . newly married . . . to be excused from duty for one year."

$W$hy don't we revive this marriage practice? A year-long honeymoon, free at home, exempt from all duties and business, just playing around, enjoying each other! There would be no pressures, no relatives or well-meaning friends prodding us to articulate our career goals or to assume responsibility.

All kinds of practical questions come to our work-oriented minds: Who would feed them? Who would support them? Wouldn't they get out of the habit of working? But if taking a year off were the norm, we would find a way to make it work.

Think of all the good learning that could come from a year like that. We could learn it really doesn't take much to live as our consumer society would have us believe. We could learn to communicate with each other, and might save thousands of dollars later in life by preventing the need to enroll in how-to-communicate seminars and how-to-fight-fair workshops.

Above all, we would be forced to learn how to play together. Marriages would not be as likely to die of boredom or workaholism. If duty is the only thing holding a marriage together, what happens when someone who brings a little "fun" into our life comes along? Marriages need love, work, and *fun* to survive. Let's lobby for a personal renewal of Deut. 24:5!

Lord of the dance, give us a long honeymoon.

**How much time do you spend together in play?**
**Plan your week to include time for fun, too.**

# ■ THE JERICHO PLAN

Josh. 6:20: ". . . and the walls collapsed."

$A$ wedding is a crossing of the Jordan into the promised land of marriage. But like the Israelites, who faced the 30-foot high double-thick Jericho walls soon after crossing the Jordan, newlyweds soon run into obstacles that seem impassable. The first fight, the first hurting words, the first misunderstanding, and it seems like we'll never be able to continue our journey into the promised land.

God gave the children of Israel a "Jericho plan," and following a similar plan could help newlyweds surmount their first obstacle. *Step one:* Seek personal renewal (Josh. 5:15). Each person must walk alone into God's holy presence to become aware of his or her own dirty shoes. *Step two:* Don't talk. No nagging, cajoling, or haranguing. Just be quiet and meditate on the Word of the Lord for six days.

When the seventh day comes you can be quite sure the walls will be ready to tumble! You won't be able to wait to break the silence with words of love and reconciliation. After the silence it will sound like shouting! As the walls come tumbling down, you can walk over them into a renewed and deeper relationship.

God of the impossible, break down the walls we build between us.

**It's helpful to have a plan for dealing with conflict before it arises. What's your "Jericho plan"?**

# ■ THE WIFE WHO WENT TO WAR

Judg. 4:10: ". . . and ten thousand men followed him. Deborah went with him. . . ."

How do you handle a relationship where God calls the wife to be a prophet, judge, and warrior? Apparently Lappidoth and Deborah had no problem with this since both accepted God's call to Deborah as valid. If her God-given gifts could more effectively serve the needs of the people at that particular moment in history, then somehow or other they would have to adapt to that call.

How do marriage partners subordinate their individual drives and desires when God's business interferes with domestic routines? Both Lappidoth and Deborah had to assume obligations which they may not have expected or wanted. Who wants to go to war, leaving the comforts of home and the loving presence of a spouse to endure the dangers of battle? How does one handle resentment and possible jealousy when one's mate receives more public recognition?

While many couples will probably work out their marriages in traditional roles, our complex economic and cultural situations will require a variety of adaptations to each other's vocational demands. We will all have to make personal sacrifices in the process. Surely Deborah and Lappidoth must have spent a great deal of time praying and talking in order for their marriage to survive the strain of God's extraordinary demands.

Beckoning Lord, give us wisdom and courage to live out our callings.

**What adjustments have you had to make to each other's vocational demands? How do you handle feelings of competitiveness?**

# ■ BEYOND THE CALL OF DUTY

Ruth 2:8-13: "You have made me feel better by speaking gently to me" (v. 13).

Nothing is more demeaning than to be dependent on the charity of others. Ruth, as a penniless and childless widow, was in that position. If her dead husband's relatives had refused to help her, her situation would have been hopeless.

Kinship laws required Boaz to take Ruth into his home if her nearest kinsman (who remains unnamed in the story) did not want to fulfill his obligation. When he refused, Boaz did not take advantage of Ruth's dependent condition. Nor did he grudgingly do his duty toward her. Rather he saw to it that she had extra grain to gather when she came to reap leftover barley from his fields; he invited her to share his own lunch, and warned his reapers not to molest her.

Picture the responding love that a man like Boaz must have kindled in Ruth's heart! On his part, his marriage proposal was prompted by more than duty. It was his response to the person she was—a woman of courage and moral goodness, one who was not afraid to press her rights as a kinswoman but did so with grace and humility.

Too often duty is invoked to keep marriages going. Boaz and Ruth show us a better way. Theirs was a union of mutual respect and admiration.

Lord, help us to keep duty from becoming a substitute for love in our marriage.

**What difference does it make if we fulfill obligations out of a sense of duty or out of love?**

# ■ AREN'T I NUMBER ONE?

1 Sam. 1:8: "Don't I mean more to you than ten sons?"

It isn't enough for a marriage just to last. It's what a relationship ends up looking like that matters.

Two older couples were eating in a restaurant. One couple touched hands and made frequent eye contact as they ate and talked. The others were absorbed in eating, and left without ever having talked or looked at each other. Which couple would you rather grow to be?

Elkanah's cry reminds us that a couple's relationship is primary and ongoing. After all, *we* left our parents and any children we have will leave *us*, but the relationship of husband and wife continues.

When children or work take the place of a spouse, trouble is brewing. Elkanah's question expresses the anguish of a spouse who feels displaced in his mate's affections. When Hannah cried all the time and refused to eat, Elkanah could not understand why his love for her was not enough. After all, *he* loved *her* even though she was childless. Apparently that love of his was deep enough to sustain him in spite of his troubled feelings. Understanding for Hannah came later when she relinquished their son to the Lord.

A marriage will be satisfying in the end only if we have worked along the way at keeping our spouse number one in our affections.

Lord, keep us from putting any other human relationship before each other.

**How do you feel when you think someone or something else has a higher priority than you in your spouse's affections?**

# ■ PLEASE DON'T LOOK DOWN ON ME

2 Sam. 6:16: ". . . and she was disgusted with him."

Michal was David's wife and the daughter of King Saul. Brought up as a royal princess, her childhood had probably been shaped by warnings like "Don't do that! What will people think?" Every spontaneous and childlike act was probably squelched to squeeze her into the royal mold.

Then came David, her shepherd-king husband, leaping and dancing as he brought the sacred ark of the Lord into the city of Jerusalem! "But kings don't do things like that, David! The servant girls will laugh at you!" All of the criticism that had restricted her freedom in childhood rose up in Michal to condemn David. In her heart she was disgusted with her husband.

Is anything more destructive to a relationship than a critical spirit? Probably not. Often someone who has been severely criticized as a child will replay those critical "parent tapes" as an adult, denying a spouse any right to express spontaneous joy. "What will people think?"

Michal's critical spirit killed David's love for her and only made him more determined than ever to be what she despised (6:22). Watch out when you tell your mate something that starts this way: "I'm only telling you this for your own good. . . ." A criticism is on its way. It won't change your mate; it will just turn love into hate.

Lord, help us to be lovers of each other and not judges.

**Talk about the feelings you experience when your spouse does something you find embarrassing. Where do those feelings come from?**

# ■ THE GAME NO ONE WINS

1 Kings 11:3: "Solomon married seven hundred princesses and also had three hundred concubines."

In Solomon's day collecting lovers was a game only men could play. Today anyone can play. Money, time, a high need for approval, and a low concern for God's moral law are all that's required to get in the game. Willing partners are usually readily available.

Now the last verses of chapter 10 in 1 Kings tell us just how shrewd Solomon was, but for a smart man he was rather stupid in his interpersonal relationships. He could not resist collecting horses, money, and women.

Philanderers are often victims of low self-esteem. The shadow of his father lay heavily over Solomon's reign. David was the beloved of the Lord, and no matter how successful, rich, or wise Solomon was, he could never match the charisma of the shepherd boy with the slingshot. David was the chosen one; Solomon was just the inheritor.

Philanderers may also be sociopaths who use people as things for their own pleasure. What man could possibly care about the individual needs of a thousand women? They were simply collector's items.

Solomon paid a terrible price for his sin. His wives used *him* to propagate their own religious beliefs, and the Lord's anger tore his kingdom away from him (1 Kings 11:9-11). The temptation to flirt invites us all to the game no one wins. For Solomon the price was one thousand frustrated and conniving women and rejection by God!

Lord, help us not to be users and betrayers of other people.

**Do you ever feel used by your lover? When? What do you do about it?**

# ■ GOD'S OPEN HOUSE

2 Kings 22:14: "Hilkiah . . . went to consult a woman named Huldah, a prophet."

Where do you go when you have a problem and need to talk to someone? Do people ever come to you? There are certain homes that seem to draw people with problems. In such a home there is often someone through whom God speaks words of wisdom and prophetic insight.

The home of Huldah and Shallum was like that. Everyone knew their address: the newer part of Jerusalem. When King Josiah told the priest Hilkiah to find out what God meant in a certain passage of the book of the Law, Hilkiah knew exactly where to go to make inquiry. He went to Huldah, the prophet of the Lord.

How many times a day were Huldah and Shallum interrupted by people wanting a "word from the Lord?" Every day was open house for them. Shallum must have been somewhat awed by his wife's immediate access to the mind of God and by the kings and priests who sought her counsel. But he was wise enough not to deny her the use of her gift.

What does it take to have that kind of home? Nothing indicates their home was unusual, but there is every indication that the people living in it were unusual. The fire of prophecy burned in Huldah, and Shallum fanned the flames with his loving support. Together they warmed the hearts of all who came to their open house for God.

Let our homes, Lord, be open to all who seek a word from you.

**What is the reputation of your home? What do others look for there?**

27

# ■ A LOAF OF BREAD

1 Chron. 16:2-3: "He gave each man and woman in Israel a loaf of bread" (v. 3).

Women are just about invisible in the chronicler's record. That history of Israel is dedicated to the memory of men, their sons, and their grandsons. Sometimes it seems that if women had not been needed to bear those sons and grandsons the chronicler might not have mentioned them at all. Daughters remain nameless and without mention until we come to chapter 16.

If human history fails to record our names, God remembers. If society ignores whole segments of God's people, God notices them. In the presence of the ark of God, everyone is included. *God is for everyone!* David knew that, so he ordered men and women to receive exactly the same portions: a loaf of bread, a portion of meat, and some raisins.

Seekers will find the riches of the Scriptures. Just as we were ready to skip Chronicles in this book because we could find nothing that applied to couples, we found what we sought. Like small raisins themselves, these verses were hidden in 1 Chronicles! In worship women and men were brought together and given the same portions of God's gifts.

Satisfied, all the people departed to their homes (v. 43) to share their gifts. Go in peace. Serve the Lord.

Caring God, we thank you for satisfying both of us with your gifts.

**How would you feel if 1 Chronicles never mentioned women?**

# ■ WHEN EQUALS MEET

2 Chron. 9:12: "King Solomon gave the Queen of Sheba everything she asked for."

All the kings of the earth came to hear the wisdom of Solomon (9:23), but the monarch who got the lion's share of his time was the Queen of Sheba. She came "to test him with difficult questions" (9:1), and Solomon responded to her toughness.

Nothing fascinates us more than meeting an equal, someone who can discuss the subjects we enjoy, who can beat us at our own games (sometimes), who has seen the places we have seen, and whose intelligence matches our own. What a sparkling meeting of mind and spirit!

That's the way it was with Solomon and his visitor from Sheba. She had come a long way just to see if the man matched the legend. He did, and his answers to her questions fascinated her. In turn, she so intrigued Solomon that he gave her everything she wanted.

What sort of woman was she, this Queen of Sheba? Jesus talked about her, saying she would rise up in the judgment to accuse unbelievers, because he was greater than Solomon (Luke 11:31). Is it possible that she, like Abraham, saw the time of Jesus' coming and was glad (John 8:56)?

We can only guess what might have passed between Solomon and the Queen of Sheba, but when two people who respect each other as whole persons come together, exciting sharing takes place!

God of wisdom, enrich our dialog with shared insights from you.

**List topics that make your conversation sparkle.**
**What interests do you have in common?**
**What different viewpoints stimulate discussion?**

# ■ THE GREAT DIVORCE

Ezra 10:44: "All these men had foreign wives. They divorced them and sent them and their children away."

The course of young love never ran smooth for Israelites who fell in love with persons of foreign nations. The fault lay not in their racial backgrounds, but in their gods. What did the God of the Ten Commandments have in common with gods who encouraged temple prostitution and the sacrifice of little children?

Ezra was a tough law-and-order man. Even so, how could he justify the massive heartbreak of women and children who were cut off from their husbands and fathers, their sources of support? Did he even try to make converts of the foreign women? Do two wrongs make a right?

The rigidity with which the law was enforced by Ezra reminds us again of the enormous debt we owe to Jesus Christ. He broke down all the walls that formerly separated races, classes, and the sexes (Eph. 2:14-18). Warnings are given against marrying unbelievers, but the New Testament also assures us that an unbelieving partner is made acceptable to God by a believing spouse (1 Cor. 7:14).

The love that God gives enables those of different backgrounds to live together in peace. Thank God that free societies no longer force anyone to send away women and children because they are of the "wrong" faith!

Jesus, breaker of barriers, help us to affirm our differences.

**What differences could divide your union? How do you overcome them?**

# ■ READ, WEEP, AND REJOICE

Neh. 8:9-10: "The joy that the Lord gives you will make you strong" (v. 10).

Do you tell each other daily, "I love you"? Does the memory of past loving acts make you cherish each other more?

The "book of the Law" (Deuteronomy) was read regularly to remind the people of God's past kindnesses. His mercies were their inheritance and his acts on their behalf were milestones in their history: liberation from slavery in Egypt, manna in the wilderness, the gift of a homeland, and a return from captivity. The people wept as the book was read.

Do you weep when you recall the loving acts of God in your marriage?

• The time you saw no possible way to save your marriage and God opened a door?

• The time you feared for your mate's life but God gave healing?

• The sin that threatened to destroy your relationship but was confessed and forgiven?

When you think of God's past mercies you may weep like the Israelites. Ezra urged them to turn their tears into rejoicing. "The joy that the Lord gives you will make you strong," he told them.

Kind deeds freely performed by a loving spouse when we least merit them bring tears of joy in their wake. Those tears become a wellspring of strength, enabling us to carry on.

> God, your mercies overwhelm us! We praise you for countless acts of kindness through the days of our years.

**What remembered acts of love from your mate bring tears of joy? Share them.**

# ■ THE DARING OF LOVE

Esther 4:10-16: ''I will go to the king, even though it is against the law'' (v. 16).

$W$hy is it so difficult to bring requests to the one you love? So often our voices betray our fear with shrillness or whining. A husband may feel obliged to ply his wife with flowers or candy when he wants something from her, and a wife may become manipulative and coy to get her way.

We know we have power over each other. Men often hold economic advantage over their wives; women sometimes gain emotional advantage over their husbands. We hold the power to destroy each other if we will.

King Xerxes wielded life and death power over Esther. His displeasure meant the end of her life. When she confronted him with her request, she was really risking everything.

Where do you find the wisdom and strength to bring up a subject that you know might cause a flare-up of anger from your spouse? How do you confront unpleasant but necessary matters?

Esther asked her friends to fast and pray with her when she saw the showdown coming. Involving God's Spirit opens the way to your mate's heart. But go only to trusted friends who have been tested through experience, and don't tell them your marital problems unless you absolutely know you need help. Too much public disclosure can ruin a marriage.

Love made Esther daring, and faith made her trust God to open the way to her lover's heart.

God, teach us loving ways to confront one another when necessary.

**How do *you* get things that bother you out in the open?**

## ■ WHEN YOU JUST CAN'T TAKE ANY MORE

Job 2:9-10: ''Why don't you curse God and die?'' (v. 9).

Cursing God seems like a perfectly natural reaction on the part of Job's wife! After all, her ten children were all killed in a tornado, enemies stole their work animals and killed all of their employees, and "fire from heaven" burned up everything else. On top of all that her husband was covered from head to toe with loathsome sores!

Touching, holding, loving—all were unavailable when she most needed them. Hell couldn't be much worse, so why not curse God and be done with it? Wasn't life over for this couple anyway?

Inevitably loss brings grief, and grief brings anger. Anger screamed inside Job's wife against God and against her passive husband sitting on an ash heap, patiently scraping his sores while she was going crazy with loneliness and grief. Out of her anguish came her terrible cry.

Love helps us look beyond another's words. Job told her to stop speaking like a foolish woman, but he did not call *her* foolish. He seemed to know that by her ability to articulate her own feelings of anger she was keeping him from saying something against God. We know he had great bitterness in his heart (see 7:11), but her cries enabled him to reaffirm his faith. He reminded her that all of their good things had come from God in the first place.

Lord, give us enough love to see the pain behind each other's anger.

**Have you ever said hurting things to your partner out of your own hurt?**

# ■ TURNING WORDS INTO CONVERSATION

Ps. 107:19-20: "He healed them with his command" (v. 20).

In all too many cases, couples exchange many words but have little conversation. Grocery lists are composed, tax information exchanged, relatives' problems discussed, spectacular news items delivered, but little sitting-down-with-nothing-else-to-do conversation happens.

An obsolete definition of "to converse" is "to have sexual intercourse." Since the 17th century, "to converse" has meant talking with another. Many women complain that their husbands rarely talk at all, and hardly ever make "verbal love" to them. A "smooth talker" deserves his stereotype as a seducer, since many women find sweet talk more arousing than physical foreplay.

Read this psalm with its list of afflictions, and notice that when emotional and spiritual healing is required, God sends forth his word. Words heal. They say the things we need to hear in order to sustain the conviction that we are loved. God tells us he loves us and backs up his words with his actions.

The kind of healing talk which marriages need has to do with feelings, not facts. Conversation of this nature performs the same function as physical caressing. It strokes us. It says we are worth listening to; our opinions and feelings are important to the one we love.

Word of God incarnate, give us healing words for each other.

**List the words of endearment you reserve for each other. When you hear them, how do they make you feel?**

# ■ POLISH EACH OTHER'S GIFTS

Prov. 31:16: "She looks at land and buys it."

The give-and-take of marriage comes to life in this remarkable tale of a radiant relationship! Each one gave permission for the other's fullest development.

*She* farmed, manufactured, managed servants and a household, organized business ventures, and was an entrepreneur. *He* served as an elder and a judge sitting in a seat of authority in their city.

This unnamed couple provided a supportive base for each other. Each polished, caressed, and encouraged the other's gifts. Living out their God-given potential in a competition-free environment produced a home of sheer delight. Fed by one another's loving praise, their amazing abilities were fully utilized.

This man and woman could each survive and do well independent of each other, but they chose to combine their energies to produce a whole that was greater than the sum of its parts.

Marriage models like this free us to share responsibilities maturely. Many of the mothers in America are employed outside the home just as this ancient mother was. "Her children show their appreciation, and her husband praises her." In turn "she does him good and never harm" (Prov. 31:12, 28). What a marriage!

Lord, free us from competition to live in a mutually supportive way.

**How do you help each other identify and use your abilities?**

# ■ OH, WHAT A BORE!

Eccles. 1:8-9: "There is nothing new in the whole world" (v. 9).

Our marriage is so dull! I know what my spouse is going to say before it's said. I know exactly when and how we're going to make love. All the romance is gone!" Have you ever felt that way? Said it out loud?

Nothing new under the sun. A marriage with a bad case of "the blahs." Times like that can come to every relationship. We get caught up in the routines of every day, and the excitement of the honeymoon drains away in those mundane activities.

When disillusionment and boredom characterize a marriage, the partners may be dwelling too much on the tingling excitements of courtship days. Compared to their remembered magic, today seems so humdrum. Back then new intimacies were constantly bringing new discoveries, and shared secrets unveiled new delights.

You may think you know everything there is to know about your lover. Do you really? After all, you've changed; what makes you think your mate hasn't? Do you know the *new person* she or he has become?

People whose relationships stay exciting are those who have the insight and ability to assess their love within the context of change. They are convinced that what they have in their marriage *now* is more important and exciting than whatever it was that led to marriage *then*.

Creative Lord, help us to rediscover each other daily.

**List things about yourself that others seem to find exciting. Check your perceptions with your partner.**

# ■ THOSE LITTLE BUGGING HABITS

Song of Sol. 2:15: "Catch the foxes, the little foxes, before they ruin our vineyard in bloom."

All lovers need to read the Song of Solomon regularly, applying the words to themselves. Read it aloud like the love duet it is.

The Song's sensuous strains are momentarily interrupted by a chilling little verse, a reminder that even a love of the most heroic proportions can be destroyed by little things, by "little foxes." What are they and where do they come from, those little foxes?

Did the mighty man with thighs like "columns of alabaster set in sockets of gold" (5:15) snore and make gurgling noises in his sleep? Was that his little fox? Did she whose breasts were like "twin deer, like two gazelles" (7:3) ever pick her nose?

Some people may not be bothered at all by little things; others are eventually blinded by some little bugging habit to every good quality in the other person.

Sometimes the little foxes are not personal habits but little sins that are allowed to come into the garden of love—a lustful look at someone else's mate or the coveting of someone else's possessions. Little longing looks grow into big blinding obsessions. So catch the little foxes before they nip your blossoming marriage in the bud!

Owner of the vineyard, reveal to us the little foxes in our lives.

**What are the little things about your partner that eat away at you? What do you suppose bothers your partner about you?**

## ■ FINDING YOUR APOSTOLATE

Isa. 1:12-17: "See that justice is done—help those who are oppressed" (v. 17).

Is it enough for God if we go to church? Well, that's a good place to begin. In fact you may find yourself an "odd couple" in your apartment or neighborhood if you go to church. In this passage God is *not* putting down churchgoing or religious habits.

But the word God gave to the prophets has this recurring theme: "Forget about your religious rituals if you're going to keep on cheating the poor, robbing orphans and widows, and oppressing migrants and aliens."

God sends us out from our solemn assemblies to seek justice and correct oppression. That is our calling, our apostolate. If your worship has grown dull, your prayer life routine, your giving half-hearted, just go out and look for hurts to heal and needs to meet. You will soon find many who desperately need both the good news of Jesus Christ and concrete acts of help.

An apartment house manager wonders why no one from the church across the street has ever come to see her with an offer to minister to the lonely elders in her building; families of prisoners struggle along in isolation; single parents long for social contact. "Give orphans their rights, and defend widows" (v. 17). A hurting world needs ministry.

Couples who find a common apostolate renew their marriage and find new excitement in their lives. Your apostolate may be nearer at hand than you think.

Where in the world is our apostolate, Lord? To whom are we sent?

**Go together to your local jail or social services office. Find out where people are hurting. Discuss ways to respond.**

# ■ REWORKING A RELATIONSHIP

Jer. 18:1-4: ". . . he would take the clay and make it into something else" (v. 4).

Like a potter at his wheel, God is always reshaping his relationship with us and his world. Nothing is static in creation; we are different today than yesterday. Newspapers rework the headlines from the day before; politicians seek issues to replace those the public responded to yesterday. God's purposes stay the same and his love does not change. But the shape of his will for us conforms to the speed of the wheel and the pressure of the potter's hands.

Pressures from our changing selves and our fickle culture alter the shape of our relationships. One day's tiredness flattens them; the next day's energy spins the wheel a little faster and perks it up. The clay of our marriage fits the contours of our moods.

The divine potter does not abandon the wheel because the clay spins out of shape, nor does he throw the clay away because it collapses under his hands. Throwing it back on the rotating wheel, he molds it into another vessel.

The wheel of marriage spins on and the shape of our relationship changes. Does the change frighten you? Will you abandon the clay because the vessel is becoming different from the original plan? Put your hands together on the wheel and discover the excitement of helping to develop the direction of your life together.

Heavenly potter, put your hand over ours as we mold our marriage.

**Think of your marriage as a clay vessel. Describe the shape it's in now.**

## ■ EVERY DAY A NEW BEGINNING

Lam. 3:22-24: "The Lord's unfailing love and mercy . . . Fresh as the morning" (vv. 22-23).

Has your marriage bed ever seemed 15 feet wide? You each stay on your own side and very carefully avoid touching the other. How you long to "make up" and cross that invisible wall that separates you! But no one offers the first tender touch and no one breaks the awful silence with a loving word.

"The thought of my pain, my homelessness, is bitter poison," cried the prophet. "I think of it constantly, and my spirit is depressed" (3:19-20). Where is hope at a time like this? Hope comes when morning ends the long, dark, restless night. With the new day what seemed an irreconcilable difference in the dark yields once more to the power of love.

Every morning is a resurrection time. The sins and dyings of the day before have been buried in the darkness of night. Dawn brings new mercies out of the steadfast love of the Lord. Another day of grace, another day of possibilities, another day pregnant with new solutions. Never say never; there's always another day on the way. Like manna in the wilderness, God's grace is fresh every morning.

So sing in the shower, laugh at last night's foolishness, and reach out to touch your beloved.

Lord of all mercy, make every morning fresh and new for us.

**How do you face the day? Share ways in which you experience newness in the morning.**

# ■ TENDER LOVING CARE

Ezek. 34:11-16: "I will look for . . . bring back . . .
bandage . . . and heal" (v. 16).

Sometimes I want my lover to be my nurturing
parent. At those times I have a childlike need for
tender, loving care—longing to be held, stroked, and
comforted. Position in life does not alter those needs.
Business executives, construction workers, artists,
teachers, parents—all have a crying child inside.

God is aware of this need. Picturing himself as a
shepherd, he catalogs his activities as seeking,
rescuing, gathering, feeding, binding up, and
strengthening, all those good things that meet my
childlike needs.

Some days we slip into deep wells of depression or
feel lost in dark caverns of hopelessness. Then, my
beloved, do you care enough to come looking for me
in the dark places of my spirit, to seek me out and
rescue me from the demons of despair? And when you
are in that "far country" of loneliness and desolation,
let me be your guide back into meaningful
relationships. When we see each other cut and bruised
by our encounters in the world, let's bind up each
other's hurts and feed one another with the loving
care that's more satisfying than bread.

We'll have to renew our own supply of love daily
if we are to be sufficient for each other's insatiable need
for tender loving care. God has enough for us all.

Tender Shepherd, give us a rich supply of
tenderness for each other.

**Find a preschool picture of yourself, if possible.
What needs of that child still exist in you?
Share them with your mate.**

# ■ KINDNESS THAT KILLS

Dan. 1:8-16: "Give us vegetables to eat and water to drink" (v. 12).

Men and women who love to cook frequently kill their mates with kindness. They "cook up a storm" and make rich and massive meals the mark of conjugal love. Candy companies encourage love-gifts of chocolate Easter eggs, Christmas boxes, and Mother's Day specials! Anniversaries and birthdays are celebrated with rich cakes and lavish dining out. Holidays ritualize overeating and overdrinking.

Babylon's king was caught up in the same syndrome. Having selected the finest young people for leadership training, he provided them with rich foods from his own table in the hope that they would be of superior appearance and health. The rich foods were also dedicated to pagan deities.

Daniel's life was dedicated to the God of Israel, and his God looked for simplicity of life. Daniel asked for a diet of vegetables and water. At the end of the ten-day test period, he and his friends were in better health than those who had eaten the king's rich food. A revolutionary U.S. government study says that the death rate of Americans can be reduced 20%-55% in various age groups by the substitution of whole grains, vegetables, and fruits for foods high in fat and cholesterol.

No one who loves another would want to limit that person's life. Loving means being concerned for the *whole* person—body, mind, and spirit.

Lord of our bodies, help us to be sharers of healthy routines.

**Check your refrigerator and cupboards for "junk foods." Work out a regular exercise routine and agree on a wholesome diet.**

## ■ REMEMBERING OUR VOWS

Hos. 2:19-20: "I will make you . . . mine forever" (v. 19).

I pledge to be faithful to you." How fervently we made this promise on that unforgettable wedding day! We burned with longing to be sealed for keeps.

Broken vows, unfaithfulness, and betrayal always traumatize. If you've ever experienced these, you know how shattering is the hurt, the sense of being unwanted and unloved. Mother Teresa, whose religious order is dedicated to picking up the dying off the streets of Calcutta, affirms that being unwanted still remains life's greatest tragedy.

Hosea felt the bite of betrayal when his beloved went after other lovers, but his pain was microscopic compared to the anguish of God over rejection by the people whom he had rescued, nurtured, and made rich. But God will go to any length to keep a covenant relationship alive. Even in the face of the utter disdain shown by his people, the hoarse cry, terrible in its love, rings out: "I will win her back with words of love" (v. 14).

God-like love moves the lover beyond hurt to renewed devotion. Love like this lives in constant hope and acts to keep the relationship alive. "I will win her back"; I will do all I can. This unworldly idea can only originate in an otherworldly passion.

Dear God, help us to remember our wedding vows.

**Some couples hang a framed copy of their marriage pledge on their bedroom wall. Find and read your vows together.**

## ■ THE SPIRIT IN YOU

Joel 2:28-29: ". . . your sons and daughters will proclaim my message" (v. 28).

When you were baptized you received the gift of the Holy Spirit. This prophetic word from Joel, fulfilled on that Pentecost Day when the Spirit was poured out on all flesh (Acts 2), reminds us that God has good things in store for us.

What were you looking for when you married? A chance to leave your parents' home? Legal sex? Financial support through school? Babies? Or were you just thinking about being with that one special person?

No matter what your reasons for marrying, God threw in a bonus. Your mate brought with him or her the gift of God's Spirit. Your marriage is therefore more than two individuals living together. You are a couple in which the Spirit of God dwells corporately, a unit that often thinks and responds as one person, one "flesh." The Spirit in *me* touches the Spirit in *you,* and just as the Spirit spoke through the prophets, priests, and kings of the Old Testament, so God offers us the gift of speaking counsel to each other.

Being mated makes it possible to speak not just of the Spirit in me, but of the Spirit in *us.* If we are willing to be open and wait, prophetic insights will come from our relationship. Problems that we thought impossible of solution will be solved with agreement we never dreamed of.

What a privilege to be married to one of God's sons or daughters, in whom his Spirit lives!

Holy Spirit, let me hear you speaking through my beloved.

**When has your spouse spoken prophetically to you? How did you know?**

# ■ SPOILED BRATS

Amos 4:1: "Listen to this, you . . . cows of Bashan."

The highest divorce rates in the country are found in those counties with the highest average income. Financial pressures rank among the top causes of marital discord. Couples who survived early economic hardships break up when the pressures are off and they're suddenly eligible for unlimited credit.

Why do we think *more* is better? The competition to have "as much as" or "more than" is pretty fierce, and commercials whet our consumer appetites. We begin to notice that our appliances look out-of-date and the neighbor's lawn mower makes ours seem obsolete.

"Cows of Bashan." When that term is used to describe women it conjures up some repulsive images. Apparently the cows in Bashan grew fat on the rich, grain-producing land. Heads down, they just kept on eating, chewing their cud, and going back for more!

What kind of women were those Bashan gals? Spoiled brats who always got what they wanted? Unloved children who never had anything? Poverty kids who began to look for security in possessions? Did they destroy their husbands with their excessive demands for things? Then there are men who kill *themselves* in their drive to acquire and achieve. But Amos tells us that in our greedy acquisition of goods the poor are oppressed and the needy are crushed.

Lord, keep us from demanding more than we need from each other.

**What are your needs? your wants? How do you know when to buy?**

45

# ■ IF ONLY

Obad. 12-14: "You should not have. . . ."

If only my parents had treated me differently . . .

If only I had gone to college . . .

If only I were better looking . . .

If only I had taken that other job . . .

If only we had waited another year before marrying . . .

If only we had bought a house before prices went up . . .

Playing "if only" tapes dissipates our energy and drains our chances for happiness. It dredges up the ghosts of past mistakes to haunt our present relationships.

Obadiah's little one-chapter book tolls a gloom-and-doom requiem for the unregenerate Edomites. He recalled their past sins eight times with the refrain, "You should not have." Their obituary was written in the words, "Your pride has deceived you" (v. 3). "If only" they had done differently!

Regretting what cannot be changed or undone is a futile occupation. "If onlys" kill, but forgiveness heals all those dragging memories and sets us free to love ourselves. The playwright Arthur Miller talks about "taking your life in your arms." We need to discover our real selves, unencumbered by the past, living free of regret and confident that "the Lord himself will be king" (v. 21).

So turn off the tapes.

Lord, set us free from nagging regrets out of our past.

**Are there any "if onlys" affecting your relationship? Help each other to release them and let them go.**

# ■ WHEN YOU CAN'T HAVE YOUR WAY

Jon. 4:1-8: "I am better off dead than alive" (v. 3).

Jonah was one of those people who want their own way all the time and resort to a variety of manipulative tactics to get it. He took a boat to another city when God told him to go to Nineveh. When he finally realized God meant business, he gave in and carried God's message there. But when the mission was accomplished and God spared the repentant Ninevites, Jonah was upset. He didn't *want* Nineveh saved.

So he went out of the city and sat alone, sulking. Twice he told God, "If I can't have my own way I want to die."

Threatening to run away or to kill oneself are common manipulative devices. An honest, straightforward approach to problem-solving requires a strong sense of personal worth. When husbands or wives feel insecure or powerless in their relationship, they may use underhanded methods to gain the upper hand. Using sex as a bribe or threat is a common method. Threatening divorce, having an affair, or pretending to be ill are some other marital blackmail techniques.

God's patience and love are longsuffering, but the book of Jonah ends on a puzzling note. What *did* finally happen to Jonah? Did God's patience come to an end? Pouting, manipulative people are hard to live with. We hope Jonah learned that lesson before it was too late.

God, give us honest insight into any attempts to manipulate our mate.

**How do you feel when your spouse retreats into pouting? What do you do when you can't have things your way?**

# ■ FORGIVING AND FORGETTING

Mic. 7:19: "You will trample our sins underfoot and send them to the bottom of the sea!"

Some people are listkeepers. They mentally list everything that a spouse did wrong in the past and go through the whole list every time something happens that they don't like. "You *always* do that! Remember the time we were on our honeymoon and you . . . ." Usually the list has little resemblance to the event that triggered it, but is kept on "hold" for instant recall when needed.

God's example discourages listkeeping. He dumps the garbage we bring to him into the "depths of the sea."

Forgetting is hard work, but one way we can assist the process is by *not* keeping and recalling lists of past wrongs done to us. When something happens that triggers your memory of similar occurrences in the past, force yourself to stick to the present event. Don't dredge up the past garbage; stay with the here-and-now. What's happening *now?* Why am I upset *now* (not why was I upset on our honeymoon, last year, or a month ago)?

The only way to get a constantly recurring situation under control is to deal with what is happening *now.* Lists from the past simply confuse the issue and become a technique to keep the problem from being solved.

There is no true forgiving without forgetting. Since our role as Christian lovers is to be forgivers, we have to learn to forget, too.

🎵 God, we bless you for the ability to forget!
**Do you have any lists that need to be dumped?**
**Is your spouse keeping a list that you would like destroyed?**

# ■ STEADY AS SHE GOES

Nah. 1:7: "The Lord is good; he protects his people in times of trouble."

A young husband breaks his neck in a fall and is doomed to total paralysis. A young wife, pushed by emotional pressures, loses touch with reality and is confined to a mental hospital. A vacation becomes a nightmare when a young couple is kidnapped. A husband is fired without warning when new owners buy the firm he has served for 26 years.

Job said we are as prone to trouble as sparks are to flying upward from a fire (Job 5:7). In one way or another even the best-insulated life is touched by trouble.

What keeps storms from rocking your marriage? Where is the gyroscope that keeps your relationship on an even keel? How do you keep the ship "steady as she goes"? Nahum, writing of desolation and destruction, predicts hearts will melt, knees will tremble, and faces will grow pale (2:10).

When that happens to you, remember that the Lord "takes care of those who turn to him" (1:7). Everything that happens to us must pass through his hands, and nothing happens without his permission. Help will come from the most unexpected sources; friends will be found in unlikely people.

The Lord is a stronghold in the day of trouble, the gyroscope that enables your marriage to ride out the storm, "steady as she goes."

Lord, thank you for remembering who we are and what's happening to us.

**What do you expect to feel when you turn to God in times of trouble? What if you don't feel anything?**

49

# ■ JOY'S MAGIC

Hab. 3:17-18: "Even though . . . the cattle stalls are empty, I will still be joyful."

If you like reading poetry you will love Habakkuk. Try an oral reading, with one of you taking Habakkuk's lines and the other responding with God's answers. Note the imagery throughout, and the familiar words in 2:4.

As you read you may find yourself wondering how up-to-date the concepts are. Why does evil go unpunished? Haven't you asked that question many times? Why do the *more* wicked often seem to be punishing the *less* wicked? But God's promises are still valid and comforting.

No section of the book is lovelier than 3:17-18. Although the imagery is rural, city dwellers will not fail to catch its message of utter devastation. It pictures moments of quiet desperation, life caught in a constricting web, a worker trapped in the boredom of routine tasks. Breathtaking fear, sudden pain, and the cry of a hungry child are all captured in its lines.

But the whole poem is prelude to an exuberant phrase that leaps off the page like a crashing cymbal: "I will still be joyful and glad, because the Lord God is my savior" (v. 18).

Joy's magic lies in the promised presence of God. You may be in the shadow for the moment, but God's light will be the final answer. Everything may seem lost for the present, but "the time is coming quickly, and what I show you will come true. It may seem slow in coming, but wait for it" (2:3).

Lord of all joy, thank you for the rejoicing that blossoms amid desolation.

*Practice* rejoicing. The words "I will" (3:18) indicate a conscious act.

# ■ RENEWED BY LOVE

Zeph. 3:17: "in his love he will give you new life."

The word *love* is never clearly defined in the Bible. But its meaning is made clear in God's saving acts and his unrelenting pursuit of the welfare of his people. Like the invisible energy of an electric current, love has the power to renew, restore, and revitalize.

In situations of pain and loss the warmth of a lover's body pressing close is more comforting than many words. When we hold one another and make love we express the inexpressible. Love is the pacemaker that forces the crushed heart to beat again.

The fire of sexual love wards off death's chill as the years move on, reminding us that love and life have the last word. Love has power to end "the threat of doom" and turn "shame to honor" (vv. 18-19). How many alcoholics have found their way back from shame to honor because their lover was willing to walk the road with them? How many victims of disabling diseases, mutilating surgeries, scarring accidents, or wars have become whole persons again because the love of a mate made them feel beautiful once more?

Our love takes shape as we imitate God. Through our actions the inexpressible is expressed and our lives are renewed.

 God of love, give us renewing love for each other.

**Tell your spouse how his or her love renews you. Can you recall a specific time when this happened?**

# ■ OUR LITTLE WORLD

Hag. 1:9: "every one of you is busy working on his own house."

It gets harder and harder to get work done around the house. With skyrocketing housing costs, both of you probably have to work outside the home. That means doing house and yard work in the evenings and on weekends, to say nothing of washing the car(s), visiting parents, shopping, washing clothes, etc., etc., etc.

Do you sometimes feel your life is a frustrating rat race? You got married to be together, to enjoy each other's company, and now you find you have time for little except work.

How intriguing to learn that this was the situation in Haggai's day, too, over 500 years before Christ! Folks then must have felt much the way many do now: working people "cannot earn enough to live on" (v. 6). All the hard work seems to accomplish so little.

Haggai says you've got to get your priorities right, and the first priority must be the building of God's house. As long as our commitments there have not been taken care of, nothing else prospers and "nothing can grow" (v. 10). But when the foundation of the temple was laid, the word of the Lord came: "from now on I will bless you" (2:19).

There will never be enough time for all the things we have to do in order to live. If you're going to get anything done, you'll have to *make* time.

God, there's always so much to be done. Set our priorities straight.

**Make a list of all the things the two of you have to do. Then rank them as to their importance. Decide who will do what, and when.**

# ■ PRISONERS OF HOPE

Zech. 9:9-12: "Rejoice. . . . your king is coming to you!" (v. 9)

$W$e draw near to the end of the Old Testament with a sense of relief. Reading all of the minor prophets at one time can be a depressing experience, like reading a newspaper obituary column the day after a tornado has gone through your city or a flash flood has wiped out your town.

Is today a "minor prophet" day in your life? Does your personal weather forecast say "stormy weather ahead"? Are storm clouds gathering on the horizon and heading your way? Does the oracle in Zech. 9:1 seem to be speaking directly to you? Does it seem as though God "has decreed punishment" for you?

The first break in a couple's communication, the first disagreement, or the first overdrawn bank account can make a marriage appear headed for disaster. Every succeeding problem may intensify the feeling of hopelessness. A "minor prophet syndrome" can threaten our lives to the point where we "knock on wood" even on good days! Like the ancient Greeks we begin to believe that the gods are jealous of happy humans.

Not every day is a sunny one, but when that longed-for break in the clouds never seems to come, we need to focus on Zechariah's summary of history. Our King is coming! Rejoice! Praise God! Shout aloud! Even in the wind, the flood, and the fire we can become prisoners of hope. Jesus is here! The Lord has saved us!

Thank you, God, for sending the Son to shine in our lives.

**What is your personal weather forecast for today? Describe your personality generally in terms of the weather.**

# ■ PUTTING GOD FIRST

Mal. 3:6-12:  "Is it right for a person to cheat God?" (v. 8).

Did you get a good "deal" when you bought your car or house? Most of us are pretty careful with our money. It passes through our fingers too quickly, and we don't want to see it wasted.

But with all of our budget-watching, we can easily forget the true source of our income. We would not have any of our money or possessions if God had not given them to us. God loves us and wants our needs to be met. But he also insists that we use our gifts to help others in need.

The people of Malachi's time were much like us. They were wrapped up in their own finances, and stopped returning a portion of their produce to God. God's response was sharp and to the point: "I ask you, is it right for a person to cheat God? Of course not, yet you are cheating me. . . . In the matter of tithes and offerings" (v. 8). God put a curse on the entire nation for its selfishness.

Did you plan your budget when you married? What portion of your income did you set aside for God? Does it reflect the priority he has in your lives? Jesus said, "your heart will always be where your riches are" (Luke 12:34). We can identify our priorities by the amount of money we actually spend on them. If God is our number one priority, we will not forget to share a portion of our income with the church, the poor, and the hungry.

Lord, give us the courage and faith to put you first.

**Talk about your commitment of money to God's work. Does it reflect your priorities?**

# ■ ADAPTING TO THE OTHER'S AGENDA

Matt. 1:18-25: "Joseph . . . married Mary, as the angel of the Lord had told him to" (v. 24).

What if your occupations take you in opposite directions? What if one of you wants to move and the other doesn't? Whose desire comes first? Which one should take priority?

The traditional answer was, "the husband's agenda comes first." Many states still have laws dictating that a woman must be officially "domiciled" at her husband's address—even though they may be working in different cities. As more and more couples enjoy dual careers, alternate models for decision making can found in Scripture.

Mary and Joseph found themselves in a similar predicament. How could she, a woman in a culture which said women could not even be taught the Scriptures, convince her husband-to-be that God had given her a calling which would take priority over everything else in their lives?

God intervened, and Joseph submitted to Mary's agenda. As a result, Mary's ministry was fulfilled, a ministry Joseph might have hindered by insisting on his legal rights. Joseph's greatness lies in his submission to God's will for his beloved. It doesn't matter who takes the lead, as long as God is glorified in and through our mutual ministries.

God may not send an angel to tell us what to do when we are tugged in different directions, but concern and love for each other will bring us to mutually satisfactory decisions.

Lord of our agendas, help us to be sensitive to your will.

**How do you make decisions when life presents you with different options?**

# ■ A LOVE TRIANGLE

Matt. 18:19-20: "For where two or three come together" (v. 20).

The triangle is an enduring and dramatic literary theme. The intrusion of a third person, either male or female, into a marriage can become a catalyst that changes its dynamics from trust to jealousy, from joy to pain. "Two is company, three's a crowd," we say.

But Jesus tells us about another kind of triangle, one that is healing, wholesome, and energizing. "Where two or three come together *in my name*," he affirms, "I am there with them."

Three Christians in a triad form one of the most supportive and helpful interpersonal configurations possible. The model for this grouping is found in the very nature of the triune God.

This is how the triad works: one person speaks, one listens, and the other observes and reflects. After the speaker has full opportunity to be heard and responded to, the pattern shifts. The one who was the listener may wish to tell his or her story, while the one who spoke may become the observer, and the one who observed may assume the active listening role. The group dynamic flows in a natural exchange of roles. Each person in some way represents God, who at certain times in our lives is a speaker, listener, and reflector. The living Christ is present at all times when Christians gather in his name. The power of his presence in each person can heal, comfort, arbitrate, and energize the others.

Triune God, thank you for modeling a holy triangle in your person.

**Your marriage is a "dyadic" relationship which is blessed by God. Have you ever felt the need for a supportive triad?**

# ■ FEMININE INTUITION

Matt. 27:17-19: "in a dream last night I suffered much on account of him" (v. 19).

Americans pride themselves on being intelligent, logical people. Mysticism, hunches, dreams, visions, and psychic phenomena make us uncomfortable.

Some take "feminine intuition" for granted. The implication may be that women are not logical, and intuition is appropriate to those who are emotional and irrational. But we must question any stereotype that women are "less logical" or men "less intuitive."

In the tragic story of Pilate and Jesus we see there can be good reason for listening to our mate's intuitive insights, especially when they bear testimony to our own convictions. Pilate was uncomfortable about the trial of Jesus, and really felt like throwing the case out of his court. He sensed that Jesus' accusers were bringing charges against him out of envy. The message from his wife convinced Pilate that he was right.

Have you ever noticed how often you and your mate think alike or have the same feelings about things? It pays to listen carefully to each other's intuitions. We can't always figure things out logically, and missing pieces to puzzling dilemmas often must be supplied through that mysterious sixth sense.

God's Spirit was certainly speaking through Pilate's wife the day of Jesus' trial. He should have acted more forcefully on her advice.

Lord, we are overawed by the many ways you speak to us through each other.

**When have you acted on intuition without other evidence and been right? Which of you seems to be more intuitive?**

# ■ MARRIED FOR KEEPS

Mark 10:2-12: "Man must not separate, then, what God has joined together" (v. 9).

Nervous tension at weddings is frequently dispelled by joking comments like "this one is good enough for my first" or "if this one doesn't work I can always try again." The joke may contain more truth than humor. After all, the divorce rate keeps climbing.

Although the impression is given that American marriages are of short duration, it's encouraging to note that a couple marrying today can statistically expect about 35 years of marriage before the relationship ends through death or divorce. Even with today's high divorce rate, the average married person can expect to spend about half a lifetime with one partner. Because of greater life expectancy and earlier marriage, most young couples today will remain in their marriage relationships longer than their grandparents.

Of course people *do* change and situations *do* affect relationships. The most dedicated partnerships sometimes dissolve. But God's dream for married people is permanence. Marriage is for keeps. Your pledge has no hidden clauses or fine print conditions attached. You make a 100% investment in the contract.

The key to permanence lies in the fact that marriage is God's idea, and he has joined you together. God's investment in your marriage is greater than yours. Trust him to make the days and years of your lives rich and satisfying.

 God of everlasting covenants, make our union permanent.

**Was there ever a time when you felt like breaking your covenant? What factors keep your commitment alive?**

# ■ PLAYING "LOGS AND SPECKS"

Luke 6:41-42: "First take the log out of your own eye . . ." (v. 42).

I misplace the car keys and immediately ask my mate, "What did you do with them?" After grumbling and fussing for a while, I locate them where I put them—in one of my coat pockets. Sheepishly I mumble something about finding them, saying as little as possible about where they were. But if it had been my *mate's* fault, wow!

One of our biggest assignments as married lovers is to throw out all the games people play. Jesus identified one of the most common games as "logs and specks." Remember that game you used to play as children, where the object was to hang the other player? Every time you lost a point your opponent added one more line to a stick figure hanging by a noose.

"Logs and specks" also has the object of hanging the other person. All I need to do is score enough points by proving you're always to blame and I'm never wrong. The game's been around a long time, ever since Adam and Eve started passing the buck. They wanted to escape the consequences of their sin and make themselves look good in God's eyes.

The game-playing ends when we face the fact that "everyone has sinned and is far away from God's saving presence" (Rom. 3:23). But God loves us anyway. We can freely admit that we goof. No longer do we have to pick at our mate to prove we're better than he or she is. The fun goes out of playing "logs and specks."

Lord, keep us honest with each other and ourselves.

**What's your version of "logs and specks"?**

# ■ CREATE YOUR OWN PARADE

Luke 19:28-40: "They . . . found everything just as Jesus had told them" (v. 32).

Jesus never blamed anyone else for what happened to him. He took responsibility for his own actions. *He* decided to whip the money-changers in the temple; *he* decided to go to Jerusalem; *he* laid down his life. Having made up his mind, no one could divert him from a course of action.

In Luke's account of Palm Sunday we see that Jesus even created his own parade! He told two of his disciples where to find the colt and what to do with it. When the crowd saw the disciples throwing their garments on the road in the path of the Lord, they got the idea and the parade was on! Jesus seemed to be saying that even with a cross looming ahead, praise and celebration were possible.

It's so easy to blame our troubles on others—our parents, our partner, environment, childhood, poverty, or whatever. Maybe you have to create your own parades! How about,

- eating hot dogs by candlelight,
- throwing an "autograph-my-broken-leg-cast" party, or
- running barefoot in a park?

Don't sit around waiting for someone to do something nice for you. You can create your own parade!

Lord, you give us such beautiful examples of how to live. Praise you!

**The heavier the cross, the more you need a parade. If you need one, plan one.**

## ■ MARRIAGES ARE NOT MADE IN HEAVEN

Luke 20:27-35: "men and women . . . will not then marry" (v. 35).

It depends on where you are coming from whether you like this passage or not. If marriage has not dealt kindly with you, then you may be quite happy that there will be none of it in heaven. On the other hand, those who have loved and been loved in marriage may object strenuously to its absence in heaven.

C. S. Lewis compared our inability to comprehend any heavenly ecstasy superior to sexual love to a small boy who sees his sister and her fiancé sitting on a couch eating candy and assumes the look of joy on their faces is due to the sweets they are consuming. At his age he knows of no joy greater than that of eating a whole box of candy!

But knowing our Lord Jesus Christ brings us a joy far greater than sex. Paul told the Corinthians that he had once been caught up "to the highest heaven" and there experienced things which "cannot be put into words" (2 Cor. 12:2-4). And Moses came down from Mount Sinai with his face shining so brilliantly with the glory of God that he had to wear a veil (Exod. 34:29-35).

If you have known such moments in your walk with God, then you do not need to grieve over the loss of marital union in heaven. In its place will be something so inexpressibly wonderful that sex is by comparison nothing more than a box of candy.

We stand on tiptoe, Lord, waiting for our heavenly union.

**How does the thought of a heaven without sex make you feel?**

## ■ WINE FOR YOUR WEDDING

John 2:1-11: "But you have kept the best wine
until now!" (v. 10).

According to John's gospel, Jesus performed his first
miracle at a wedding. That is very intoxicating news
for couples! We are important people to our Lord.

Think about it. Jesus had just been baptized,
anointed with the Spirit, and identified as God's Son.
He had called his disciples, and the first act he
performed as evidence of his new vocation was to
go to a wedding! There he rescued the bridegroom
from the disgraceful dilemma of not providing enough
wine for his guests.

While we cannot here tackle the problem of
alcoholism and its disastrous effects on marriage
relationships, it's important to note that Jesus did
not discourage the use of wine at this celebration.
People had drunk "freely" when the Lord's best wine
was made available.

Was Jesus making a particular theological statement
by letting this be his first sign, evidence of his glory?
Was he acknowledging a special intercessory role for
his mother? Is there significance to the fact that the
wine was created in stone jars reserved for Jewish
rites of purification?

Or was Jesus simply saying that weddings are to be
celebrated with all the jubilation and festivity
possible? The presence of Jesus in our marriage is a
possibility every day, making every moment a
sanctified celebration. Send him an invitation!

Jesus, we invite you to our marriage to share
our sacramental wine.

**Share a little bread and wine and invite Jesus to your
own private love feast.**

## ■ DEATH'S END

John 11:21-27: "whoever lives and believes in me
will never die" (v. 26).

If I stand beside your coffin some day, what will I be
thinking? I know the agony I will be *feeling*, but
what thoughts will possess my mind?

Have you ever talked to each other about death?
An amazing number of couples do not. A fear of
bringing up this subject keeps them from even making
out their wills. Talking about death seems to be a
marriage taboo.

In Genesis 3 we saw the mark that death scratches
on our lives. But at least right now we're still breathing.
What will happen when one of us leaves the land of
the living to be buried with the dead?

Jesus does not prevent our death. When Lazarus
died, Martha and others asked why the one who had
opened the eyes of a man blind from birth could not
also have kept his friend from dying. But death must
eventually come to each of us. The inevitability and
finality of that fact is what makes it so hard to
talk about.

What I'm going to remember if I stand beside your
coffin is that death really isn't final. When we believe
in Jesus, death is really its own end, a step into life
that's really life! Just a short separation, that's all.
Then we'll be reunited in a relationship that promises
to be more wonderful than any sexual union on earth
could ever be.

Living Lord, thank you for the promised
resurrection.

**Have you talked about your own dying and what that
will mean to your mate? Have you made out your
wills and decided where you will be buried?**

# ■ IT'S A SMALL, SMALL WORLD

Acts 10:34-35: "God treats everyone on the same basis" (v. 34).

The United States is unique among the nations of the world. What other country can boast such diversity? Americans are people of many colors, many languages, and many ethnic backgrounds. Living with cultural differences is commonplace.

In such a country there are naturally many cross-cultural marriages. Not too many years ago, marriages between Protestants and Catholics in some communities sparked inter-family feuds. Marriages between persons of different races were often forbidden by law. Fortunately, much of this has changed or is changing. People who have different backgrounds are coming to realize how much their lives can be enriched by learning from each other.

From God's perspective there is no problem with marriages between persons of differing cultures. "God treats everyone on the same basis." When he preached at Athens Paul pointed out that God created all from one source, and gives breath to every living thing (Acts 17:25-26).

God divides people into only two groups: those who fear him and do what is right in his sight and those who do not. *That distinction is still the most significant one for married people.* If you have a cross-cultural marriage, you know that problems can arise from your different backgrounds. But you also know that your love and faith can deal with them.

℘ Creator of us all, help us to respect our differences.

**How do your backgrounds differ culturally? What kinds of feelings do those differences bring out in you?**

## ■ TEAMMATES

Acts 18:1-3, 24-28: "they . . . explained to him
more correctly the Way of God" (v. 26).

What a team Priscilla and Aquila were! Like Paul,
they were tentmakers, but that was simply the way
they earned their living. Their true profession was
teaching the faith, and their calling was to the
missionary life.

Paul met them in Corinth and was so impressed
with their commitment and knowledge of the
Scriptures that he traveled with them. In turn they
shared their home, trade, and faith with him.

When Paul wrote to the Roman Christians he
greeted Priscilla and Aquila as his "fellow workers
in the service of Christ Jesus," saying they had "risked
their lives" for him (Rom. 16:3-4). With him they
may have fought "wild beasts" at Ephesus (1 Cor.
15:32).

What was most important was that Paul could trust
them to handle the word of God accurately. When
the eloquent preacher Apollos came to Ephesus and
taught in the synagogue, Priscilla (Prisca) and Aquila
heard him and detected incompleteness in his message,
even though he had "taught correctly the facts about
Jesus" (v. 25).

God only knows how much the ministry of Paul
was aided by these two people. Self-supporting
missionaries, Priscilla and Aquila made a terrific team!

Jesus, we want to work as a team, teaching
the word of life. Teach us, Lord.

**What about starting a couples' Bible study in your
house?**

## ■ MANAGEMENT BY VISION

Acts 26:16-19: "I did not disobey the vision I had from heaven" (v. 19).

If you don't know where you're going, how will you know what road to take or when you finally get there?

Most of us need a sense of purpose. Some dream must spur us on, some goal must beckon. Otherwise why struggle at all? Like people in rocking chairs, we generate a lot of activity and seldom get anywhere.

"Management by objective" governs the planning of many corporations. That kind of operational goal-setting is too coldly sterile for marriage, but the idea has merit. Paul knew exactly where he was going, but after Jesus met him on the Damascus road with a purpose for his life he turned around and headed in the opposite direction.

What vision sustains your marriage from day to day? How do you decide what you want to accomplish in your life together? What are your goals? Paul's goals were quite specific, attainable in his lifetime but stretching even beyond that lifetime. If he strayed from the road that led to that goal, he knew it. And when he arrived at his destination, he knew that too (2 Tim. 4:7).

The vision toward which your life together is directed must be bigger than life and beyond your grasp, or it is too meager to sustain your devotion. But the goals which propel you toward that vision must be within your grasp and attainable in your lifetime.

Almighty God, give us a vision of Jesus that will sustain us both.

**Together, write a statement of purpose for your marriage. Does your statement reflect your "heavenly vision"?**

# ■ SEX AND FANTASY

Rom. 1:26-27: "God has given them over to shameful passions" (v. 26).

Should a devotional book have such a "downer" passage in it? Maybe not in a general devotional book, but when one is directed especially to couples we'd better not pretend anything goes as long as we're married.

First of all, this passage in Romans is not about homosexuals. It's written about the evils of heterosexual people who leave their natural relationships for those which are "unnatural" for them. Most of us have fantasies of one sort or another, dreams over which we have no control and which may distress us. We may wonder where they come from if we do not usually think about such things.

Be open with one another about your fantasies. Only then can you do as Paul longed to do with the Romans: "that both you and I will be helped at the same time, you by my faith and I by yours" (1:12). You don't have to struggle alone; you can help each other. Suppressing your fantasies has a steam kettle effect. The tighter you push the lid down, the more pressure builds up from the steam in the kettle. Allowing some of the pressure to escape acts as a safety valve.

As you pray together with a spirit of acceptance and understanding, the need to act out your unnatural fantasies will diminish.

Lord, thank you for the listening love of my spouse.

**Pray with each other for the healing of your subconscious minds.**

## ■ A POWER OUTSIDE OURSELVES

Rom. 8:26-28:  "the Spirit also comes to help us, weak as we are" (v. 26).

Jingles like "when you can cope, there's hope" sound good in sermons and look good in print. Sometimes they even work.

But sometimes none of your positive (or negative) coping mechanisms work. Positive thinking, meditation, muscle relaxation, fantasizing, or jogging may take your mind off a painful situation for a while. Your favorite music or television program may distract you temporarily. But eventually the problem must be faced. Postponement may only tickle its appetite, and now there may be no escaping destruction. Even your prayers may seem to rise no higher than your own head.

That's "Spirit-time," our Scripture today tells us. Weakness becomes the channel for God's energy because "the Spirit also comes to help us, weak as we are" (v. 26). Just when we don't know how to pray is the time the Spirit intercedes for us.

A doctor says, "There's nothing more I can do," and given up for dead, a patient recovers! "You have a two percent chance of walking again," pronounces a surgeon, and soon the paralytic walks! "Your marriage is hopeless," says a counselor, and unexpected new fire begins to glow in the ashes of dead love!

We are weak, but God is strong. When we can't cope, in the Spirit there's hope.

God of the impossible, we praise you for your rescuing Spirit.

**Were you ever surprised by the Spirit when all seemed lost? Describe your feelings at that moment.**

# ■ YOU BELONG TO ME

1 Cor. 7:3-5: "A wife is not the master of her own body . . . a husband is not the master of his own body" (v. 4).

Belonging is beautiful. What satisfaction comes with saying the words, "*My* lover, *my* mate!" Even C. S. Lewis, that learned author who evidenced a certain chauvinism in his early writings, glowed with the pride of possession after his late-in-life marriage to Joy. Intimate contact with her transformed his attitudes. He was truly "surprised by Joy!"

Physical love lies at the core of every marriage. St. Paul reminds all couples that they owe their bodies to their mates—a wife for her husband's sexual needs, a husband for his wife's sexual needs. Our culture has had a fairly consistent view of male sexuality, while female sexuality has been understood in widely different ways. In the 15th century it was assumed that women's sexual needs were more urgent than men's; the 19th century discouraged sexual expression by women.

Today men and women are encouraged to be quite straightforward in their need for sexual satisfaction and to show more concern for their partner's response. According to St. Paul, this is as it should be. Sexual union is the ultimate sense of belonging, and it is sanctified in marriage. Through the union of our bodies we give ourselves to each other in joy and freedom.

Creator of male and female, thank you for the joys of sex.

**Tell each other what you enjoy about your sexual experiences.**

69

# ■ POOLING OUR RESOURCES

1 Cor. 12:4-11: "different kinds of spiritual gifts. . . . for the good of all" (vv. 4, 7).

Every Christian is gifted, a "charismatic" person. God pours out his gifts with profligate delight on all of us. One of the excitements of a loving relationship lies in the initial discovery of each other's gifts. Did you ever realize, before you married, the kind of laughter you would share in the morning? Did you catch a glimpse of your partner's tender love?

At first we are often most impressed by each other's physical charms. Like candle flames to a moth, they can attract us irresistibly. Later we begin to identify in our lover the spiritual gifts Paul listed in 1 Corinthians 12; Romans 12; Ephesians 4, and elsewhere. As life moves on, how much more valuable those gifts become than the endowments which stirred our initial longings!

As we become alive to our mate's spiritual gifts, they intensify our own and propel our life together toward new horizons. Our energies expand with divine vitality. Because one has the gift of administration, the routine cares of life are smoothly managed; because the other has the gift of helping, we both become a source of benefit to others. Marriage pools God's treasures, enriching our world!

Gift-giving Spirit, we praise you for the gift of each other's love.

**List the gifts you see in your mate. Share your lists.**

# ■ YOU CAN TRUST ME

2 Cor. 1:17-20: "For Jesus Christ. . . . is God's 'Yes' " (v. 19).

Your marriage covenant is only as good as your word. Any reason for questioning the other's honesty is the tip of a wedge that can ultimately break it. A strange female voice on the telephone asking for one's husband; a strange male visitor leaving the home during a husband's absence. Left unexplained, such insignificant and perhaps innocent events can sow the seeds of distrust.

When pretense and falsehood are *deliberately* practiced, trust may never be restored. In a relationship as intimate as marriage a double life cannot be hidden forever. The deceived spouse may choose to ignore the offense for the sake of a false peace, but the marriage union will have been destroyed. God says "anyone who . . . tells lies" will be excluded from his kingdom (Rev. 21:27).

Unreserved intimacy between lovers can grow and flourish only when yes means yes, no means no, and one's partner believes the yes and the no. Checking on the other's actions, keeping one's spouse under surveillance, or going through a mate's pockets or purse only encourages dishonesty. If the voluntary self-disclosure of one's actions brings violent responses from the other partner, then lying is encouraged.

The brittle character of trust requires careful handling from both lovers.

Lord of the yes, help us trust one another and know when we are violating trust.

**Have you ever doubted the other and been proven wrong? What is the state of your trust relationship?**

# ■ GOD ISN'T FINISHED WITH US YET

2 Cor. 5:14-17: "joined to Christ . . . a new being" (v. 17).

He'll never change!"

"She'll never be different!"

Paul said it might not be the other person that needs changing, but your own point of view. Seen from a human perspective, people often seem warped. The aspect of your mate's personality that now gnaws away at your admiration may have been the very thing which attracted you when you first met. Then you saw everything from another point of view. The aggressiveness so admired before now looks like bossiness; the flirtatiousness that once charmed you now appears to be manipulation.

What changed? Now you see each other from a human point of view. You see the bloodshot eyes, the tousled hair, and the oily skin. The heavenly vision of masculine and feminine charm you thought you saw in your courting days never really existed. That ordinary human being whom you see every day under every possible circumstance was always there. Your point of view has changed from the living room to the bedroom, bathroom, and kitchen point of view—rooms where real living has a way of reducing all of us to human size!

From Christ's point of view we are all his new creation. He just isn't finished with us yet. So let's give each other another chance!

Giver of new sight, help us see each other through Christ's eyes.

**In what ways has your mate changed since your wedding? In what ways do you think you've changed? Do you agree with each other's perspectives?**

# ■ DO YOU REALLY KNOW WHO I AM?

Gal. 2:19-20: "it is no longer I who live, but it is Christ" (v. 20).

When you were baptized into Christ you exchanged identities with him, and you will spend a lifetime figuring out everything that means. When you married, that mystery was intensified by your union. For the union of marriage has its counterpart in the mystery of the union between Christ and believers (Eph. 5:31-32).

Psychological names for aspects of personality like *id, ego,* and *superego* or *parent, adult,* and *child* sound complicated and profound, but they are elementary compared to the fact that we are people "in Christ," living out *his* life in *our* flesh.

*So you will never really know who I am, my beloved, unless you know who he is. Until then I will escape analysis or definition.*

When Matilda Bracken heard that a man named Windrow was going to carve the head of Christ from a block of oak, she said that when it was finished it would have to "cry and laugh, with every other face born human. And how can you crowd all the tragic and comic faces of mankind into one face?"

You can. "I have been put to death with Christ" (v. 19). Your face is his, and his is yours. All that we are—our life, energy, and hope—is wrapped up in that person. Our life in Christ is not just some abstract, otherworldly, vaguely spiritual concept. It's "in the flesh," right now.

Jesus, live in us, through us, and with us now, both individually and as a couple.

**What are your expectations of your mate? How do they reflect his or her humanness or "in Christ-ness"?**

# ■ A MARRIAGE OF FREEDOM

Gal. 3:27-28: "there is no difference . . . between men and women" (v. 28).

One of the reasons we have a hard time with the idea of being "in Christ" is that it changes so many of our preconceived notions, especially our notions of the social roles people are supposed to play.

We are constantly confronted with stereotypes such as "girls are girls and boys are boys." We like to fix people in immutable roles with definite distinctions. If some people don't "stay in their place" we are all too willing to give them a rough time.

Because we are in Christ, our human distinctions are erased. Husbands and wives have the exciting task of discovering mates who can't be slotted into the old role categories.

Being in Christ is *liberating*. A husband does not have to provide the sole support of his family to "be a man." A wife does not have to stay home and cook and clean all day to "be a woman." Couples may have good reason to switch roles at times.

Being in Christ is *ennobling*. None of us needs a master/slave relationship which degrades both parties. Couples can identify and utilize the talents and gifts of both husband and wife in cooperative servanthood.

A marriage free to try different roles and arrangements is possible when both partners know what it is to be in Christ. Our Lord gives us the freedom to learn what that means.

Jesus, only you can set us free from inhibiting roles. Free us, Lord!

**What roles have you chosen as marriage partners?**

# ■ NOBODY'S PERFECT

Gal. 4:12-15: "my physical condition was a great trial to you" (v. 14).

Our bodies function with intricate precision—most of the time. But lack of oxygen during the birth process, infections in childhood, acne in adolescence, or accidents at any age can affect our delicate physical mechanisms.

When we fall in love we do so with a whole person. We accept each other's imperfections as part of the loved "package."

But what if you marry with a certain set of expectations and only later discover some inherited biological weakness? What if something happens after marriage which affects one partner's appearance?

Paul had such a bodily ailment, and he knew his condition was obvious to his audience. Did he have a loathesome eye disease which they had to look at while he preached? He marveled that they "did not despise or reject" him but received him as "an angel from heaven" (v. 14).

A young woman whose husband of one year is disfigured in a fiery plane crash devotes herself tenderly to his care; a young husband who learns that his bride's sudden weakness of limb signals the onset of multiple sclerosis comforts her with redoubled compassion. And old age eventually brings physical impairment and altered appearance to all of us.

Will you be able to see an "angel from heaven" living in the changed physical features of your beloved? Your spouse will see himself or herself through your eyes and become that angel through you.

Lord, help us to give of ourselves to each other. As changes come in the other's appearance, how does it make you feel?

## ■ LIVING FREE

Gal. 5:1-6: "Christ has set us free!" (v. 1)

Has the bond of matrimony become the bondage of matrimony? Has the marriage that set you free for living and all the loving you ever wanted become a prison? Are there times when you feel trapped by love?

Marriage has the potential both to free partners for more abundant living and to bind them with invisible chains. If we deny each other any independent action, insisting on complete sharing of confidences, hobbies, and friendships, we imprison each other.

The chains are usually forged out of guilt and fear. "If you really loved me, you wouldn't *want* anyone else's company." "You always do that! I remember when you. . . ." "If you do that I'll leave!" Tears and threats lock the chains in place.

So-called "open" marriages in which the partners agree to have affairs with other persons are not the answer. Too much game-playing keeps them from ever developing true intimacy. Freedom only comes from knowing Jesus, who said "If the Son sets you free, then you will be really free" (John 8:36). Then you are liberated from possessiveness, the desire to dominate, the need to enslave or be enslaved, and the need to philander or be promiscuous.

When you know Christ's freedom no one can ever put you back under the yoke of the law again.

Lord, you have broken the chains of sin and we celebrate that freedom.

**Does your spouse do anything that makes you feel enslaved? How can you set each other free in Christ?**

# ■ WALKING THE TIGHTROPE TO MATURITY

Gal. 6:1-5: "Help carry one another's burdens" (v. 2).

Marriage is for adults and reserves its best for mature persons. The road to maturity in marriage is a tightrope stretched over the abyss of *dependence* on one side and the rocks of *independence* on the other side.

Dependency needs and the desire to be independent are at war in our natures. Healthy persons long to be cared for in some areas of their lives, but also have strengths and resources for standing alone in other areas. They're not ashamed to acknowledge both attributes.

The trick is to keep from falling completely off the tightrope on one side or the other. A wholly dependent person saps the energies of the other like a parasite. Even the strongest tree may be destroyed by a creeping fungus. A wholly independent person may crack under the effort required to prove that he or she can bear the whole load alone. In the process the other person stands by helplessly, feeling totally unneeded and unwanted.

The goal of maturity is to arrive at *interdependence,* a balance between carrying one's own load (v. 5) and always having to have one's load carried by others. Interdependence is bearing one another's burdens— not hesitating to reach out to others, but not being afraid to admit that you sometimes need help, too.

God of wholeness, help us to relate to each other out of maturity.

**Talk about areas of your life where you feel dependent and where you want to be independent. How do you relate interdependently?**

# ■ WILLING SLAVES TO LOVE

Eph. 5:21: "Submit yourselves to one another."

The focus of many discussions and lectures on marriage is "Who's boss?" Does that question ever disturb your intimacy?

According to this word to the church at Ephesus, there's only one boss in all human relationships: Jesus Christ our Lord. He does not relinquish his preeminence to anyone.

Yet Jesus' model is servanthood. Philippians 2 pictures him as giving up his position of equality with God to assume the form of a servant. Only by giving up his position of authority did he accomplish our salvation. Greatness for Christians lies in serving others.

The Bible never deviates from this standard. True stature lies not in what you take but in what you give. In marriage we are sometimes givers and sometimes receivers. Both men and women have aggressive and passive characteristics, but our society often rewards men for being aggressive and women for being passive. In so doing we have caused unnecessary pain for members of both sexes.

In a marriage between Christians, decision making should be a shared venture under the authority of Jesus Christ. All are subject to him, and husbands and wives are instructed to submit themselves to each other because of their mutual discipleship. The way of mutual submission is not an easy one, but when practiced it leads to deepening love.

Servant Lord, show us how to outdo one another in serving each other.

**Can there be a marriage which is truly 50-50 all the time? Are you willing to vary the percentages either way as the need arises?**

## ■ OBVIOUSLY CHRISTIAN

Eph. 4:30-32: "be kind and tender-hearted to one another" (v. 32).

Just reading this passage is like being massaged with warm oil at bedtime. All kinds of strokes are buried in it, waiting to be released through loving actions by loving people.

Without those loving actions we shrivel up and die. Have you ever met unloved and unloving human shells walking around your town? They may have waited too long to initiate kind deeds. We can't wait for others to reach out to us. Kind and tender actions start with us. Like a chain of upright dominos, all the barriers to love can tumble before one kind deed.

The unexpected gift of dishes washed when it was your turn to do them, the loving touch of a neck rub when you were tense and uptight, the offer of lovemaking when you were feeling lonely and uncared for—how healing these actions were to your bruised and weary spirit!

Actions, not words, reveal the real you. Love comes alive in what you *do*. Which is better, to say "I love you" and act unlovingly, or not to say the words and to act lovingly? We love to hear the words, but our actions speak more loudly. When our spouse behaves kindly and tenderly we can fill in the unspoken words ourselves because they are acting out what it means to be a Christian.

Lord, help us to be kind, tenderhearted, and forgiving of one another.

**When do you feel most "stroked" by your mate? How do you like to express your tender feelings?**

## ■ WORKING SIDE BY SIDE

Phil. 1:27-29: "with only one desire you are fighting together for the faith" (v. 27).

If opposites attract (and they often seem to), then how can you ever be of "one desire" in marriage? This develops as you work together *for* something and *against* something, for the gospel and against the enemy of the gospel.

No glue is more powerful than the sharing of common goals and common struggles. Unfortunately many couples give their energies to meager plans and puny hostilities! Soon working side by side gives way to boredom. The enemy isn't worth fighting, the goals refuse to sustain interest, and the search for new excitements is on.

Least of all does Paul's injunction to stand "firm with one common purpose" (v. 27) mean we always have to think alike. If we believe that, then we have no need to pool our Spirit-given gifts. Our diversity provides a rich matrix for creativity and stimulates many new options for living out the gospel.

Working with one desire is the outcome of a painful struggle. For two spirits to become one requires the sacrifice of one's self, the painful adjustment of one person to another. The philosophical works of Ariel and Will Durant are the result of the melding of two unique individuals into one creative whole. For over 60 years they worked side by side to spin out their books.

Can we do less for the gospel?

Make us one in the Spirit, Lord, as we work side by side.

**How are you different? How are you alike? When do you feel you are most deeply of "one desire"?**

# ■ WORRY MEDICINE

Phil. 4:6-7: "And God's peace . . . will keep your hearts" (v. 7).

You just bought a farm and hail cheats you out of your harvest. You are expecting a baby and medical research shows that a prescription you were given may injure your developing child.

When anxiety darkens the future, life's juices drain away in sleepless nights and dread-filled days. Depressants dull your mind only for a moment; consciousness brings the return of stabbing fear. You feel so alone. Even the loving embrace and tender words of your partner don't always ease your pain.

You need strong medicine, more powerful than anything humans can prescribe. God has the formula:

*Start praying,* even if you don't feel like it and don't know what to say. Tell God about your fears and exactly how you feel, without pious minimizing. Be honest.

*Describe your needs*—what you would like to have happen.

Then *start thanking God* for positive features of your situation. Hail may ruin a crop, but thank God you still have each other; medical research makes it possible to discover possible defects and the reasons for them. While you are listing things you are thankful for, even without understanding how your situation can improve, *peace and release* from anxiety will flood your heart and mind.

God of peace, thank you for medicine to ease a weary heart.

**Try applying God's "medicine" to your worried thoughts.**

## ■ LOVERS NEED FRIENDS

Col. 2:1-2: ". . . drawn together in love" (v. 2).

By rights your lover should be your best friend.
No other person knows you so well, sensing your
deepest needs and responding to them. But the
relationship between lovers is so emotionally charged
that friendship may be impossible. Love can make one
too vulnerable. Our hearts beat in our lovers' hands
and can be crushed so easily. True friendship may
not survive in such a fragile atmosphere.

The isolation of families in our country also places
great demands on a couple. Each person is expected to
fulfill many of the ego needs of the other partner.
We are made to feel responsible for each other's total
happiness, and we are looked to for fulfilling
companionship, stimulating conversation, sexual
gratification, and emotional support.

Even though the benefits of living close to our
extended families have been lost for many of us, we
still need to be "drawn together in love" with a wider
family. Christian friends bring needed objectivity to
our relationships, open new perspectives, and provide
for some of the extensive ego needs that no one human
being, not even our lover, has the power to fill. These
friends may be available only once a week in church,
by letter or by long distance telephone, but it can be a
great help to *know* that they pray for you daily.

Even lovers need friends like that.


⚙ Friend of all lovers, make us loving friends.


**Who are the friends who enrich your relationship?**

## ■ HARMONIZING HEARTS

Col. 3:16-17: "Sing . . . in your hearts" (v. 16).

Through your car radio comes the sound of music. You turn to each other with immediate recognition: "That's *our* song!" You danced to it on your first date or sang it together on your college choir tour. You chose it as the hymn at your wedding or exchanged the record for your first Christmas gift. Whenever your memory plays it back, you are drawn to your mate with renewed devotion.

Our hearts beat to many rhythms. Your own love song moves to the beat of throbbing pulses and the sudden intake of breath as your bodies meet in the universal rituals of the marriage bed.

When the word of Christ dwells in both of you it creates a melody that sings its way through your life together, a song in your hearts that enriches the rhythm of all existence. Both of you write your own lyrics to remind you of the old, old story of Jesus and his love. But your words are set to the same harmonies.

Birth and death, spring and winter, seedtime and harvest, the cross and the resurrection are the themes of God's choral anthems. They become personalized for us in believing hearts and confessing lips. The refrain "Jesus is Lord" echoes in sound waves around the world and joins the cosmic music of the spheres.

That is the song which ennobles all the other rhythms of our life and melts our hearts into one singing melody.

Composer of the song of salvation, hear our song of praise.

**What is "your song"? How do you feel when you hear it?**

# ■ WHEN WE'RE APART

1 Thess. 2:17-20:  "how hard we tried to see you again!" (v. 17)

The more we become one, the harder it is to be apart. Separation tears us in two.

Paul said the Thessalonians were his "reason for boasting" before the Lord Jesus. To be away from them for even a short time filled him with great desire to see them face to face. If friendship did this to him, how much more we who are joined in both body and spirit suffer when we are apart!

Is any bed so empty as the one which has been shared with our lover or any house more vacant than our own when our beloved is away? So deep is the hunger to be together that when death takes one partner away, the other often seeks passage on the same journey. To be without the other is somehow like being half-dead.

To minimize the loneliness of separation—to be absent "not in thoughts, of course, but only in body" (v. 17)—one can tuck little love notes in the other's suitcase to be read at journey's end. Joining hearts in prayer at the same time every day (even allowing for time zone differences) helps overcome the pain of absence. Still, great desire to see each other "face to face" grows! Like opposite poles on a magnet, nothing can keep us from being drawn together across the miles. Face to face, we live again.

God, make our separations short and our reunions frequent.

**How do you feel when your partner goes on a trip? What ways have you found to join your hearts across the miles?**

# ■ OUR LOVE KEEPS GROWING

2 Thess. 1:3: "faith is growing . . . love . . . is becoming greater."

Life would be so simple if our love just kept increasing as a matter of course. Then no one would "fall out of love," and the fires of passion would never cool. Each year we would automatically love each other more than we did the year before.

But it doesn't always work that way. Even the most compatible couples experience dry spells in their marriage. Romance yields to routine, and the rosy glow of sensual excitement dims. "What's happening to us?" is an unspoken question in both hearts. One may begin to feel sexually attracted to another person.

When you are committed to your marriage, a panicky desire to revive the old loving feeling possesses you. But the harder you work to fan the flames, the more desperate you feel. Love just won't be forced.

Paul links increasing love with growing faith. If you want your love for one another to increase, you need to focus on your relationship with the Lord. As the saying goes, "The more we love Jesus the more we love each other." That doesn't mean running to more Bible studies, attending more prayer meetings, or watching more religious telecasts. It means getting to know Jesus better through personal contact with his Word, his church, and his Spirit living in you.

Little by little we are able to say "I love you" with all our heart; once more our eyes meet with loving messages, and deeds are done that show how much we care. Love once more produces what it promises.

Loving Lord, let our love be a contagion caught by our mates.

**Plant a garden together. Watch it grow.**

# ■ IT'S OK TO BE MARRIED

1 Tim. 4:1-5: "lying spirits. . . . teach that it is
wrong to marry" (vv. 1, 3).

The institution of marriage can stand a little
promoting. Half of all couples under 30, say some
researchers, are living together without being
married. It is true that a marriage certificate may not
make much difference in many relationships, since 40%
of all first marriages and 60% of all second marriages
end in divorce. But that "piece of paper" so frequently
despised today is still the only legal method we have
for indicating our obedience to God's will that we
show respect and accept responsibility for our lover.
Even with all of its shortcomings, marriage is the most
binding contract we can make with each other
under civil law.

As all of us know, getting married does not ensure
commitment. No law on earth can *force* people to live
together if they don't want to. Nor can any law of God.

But the word to us in this Timothy passage says that
those who "teach that it is wrong to marry" are
deceitful spirits and liars. It is a good thing to be
married and make a permanent commitment. You need
not apologize for being old-fashioned, or feel like
you're missing out on a more exciting existence.

Marriage has wonderful possibilities for excitement,
ecstasy, and discovery. And it also has the blessing
of God.

You who brought the first man and woman
together, keep us committed to our marriage.

**Would you feel just as committed to your relationship
without that "piece of paper"? Why or why not?**

## ■ FEELING OK

2 Tim. 1:6-7: ". . . does not make us timid; instead . . . power, love, and self-control" (v. 7).

People who feel OK about themselves are more likely to make OK marriages, but "not OK" feelings plague so many of us. If you were always picked on as a child or told that you were dumb, stupid, lazy, or clumsy, what reason would you have for believing you could succeed at anything as an adult (such as marriage)? If you never received praise or love as a child, how could you know you were worth anything at all?

No wonder we become jealous of other people when we're sure they are better than we are. And our mate can never really convince us we're loved if we have never been made to feel worthy of love.

God does not want you to feel any of these things. In Baptism you received the Holy Spirit. You were set free from the bondage of sin, death, and the power of the devil. All your binding fears, your poor self-image, and your paralyzing sense of inadequacy were made null and void.

In the place of timidity and fear come power and love and self-control; power instead of fearfulness, love instead of self-loathing, self-control in place of panic and harmful impulses.

See what confidence returns to your relationship with your mate when you begin to appropriate God's seal of approval and power. You will sense release from the cocoon of timidity, and your marriage will be ready to fly!

Lord, help us to appropriate your promised power, love, and self-control.

**In what ways do you help each other feel OK?**

# ■ THE SPOUSE THAT REFRESHES

2 Tim. 1:15-18: "Onesiphorus . . . cheered me up many times" (v. 16).

$V$arious degrees of pious martyrdom—"holy purple hearts"—are conferred on those who stand by their friends when they have accidents, become ill, or have some reversal of their fortunes. Hardship is involved, but society approves. In fact society *disapproves* of those who abandon friends and mates at times like these.

But what about standing by each other when misfortune befalls one because he or she has championed an unpopular cause? Suppose a mate is jailed for joining a "sit-in" of welfare mothers at city hall who are protesting a cut in their meager allotment? Or suppose a spouse gets a police record for marching in a protest against nuclear weapons?

Paul was in jail for championing the cause of Jesus Christ, a crucified criminal, and for refusing to acknowledge the divinity of Caesar. When he was imprisoned some of his friends turned away. But Paul said Onesiphorus was not only unashamed that he was in prison, he "started looking for me until he found me" (v. 17).

There was nothing halfhearted about Onesiphorus' reaction, but rather a wholehearted affirmation of his friend Paul. No wonder Paul felt refreshed.

Are you able to do that for each other? Can you be a spouse who cheers up your mate? Will you be one who stays, oblivious to criticism and shame?

Lord, give us staying power for and with each other.

**Was there a time when your friends divided into two groups, those who stayed and those who abandoned you? Share that experience.**

# ■ ROOTS

Titus 3:3-7: "he saved us" (v. 5).

We seem to have very little in common with Titus and other contemporaries of St. Paul. Every generation has to work out its own destiny in the context of its particular moment in history.

Even within the same generation, circumstances differ for each of us. Like all our ancestors who preceded us, we have to draw our own road maps through a world we never made. Grandparents and grandchildren compare notes and marvel at the changes that have piled up between their childhoods. Imagine a world without television, satellites, and freeways! Was there ever a time when people did not have jet planes to carry them from place to place?

Nothing has changed more than the relationship between the sexes, and no one knows where those changes are going to take us. In a way, our situation is frightening. It was much easier to live in a world where everyone knew that a woman was either to marry and have children or go into a convent! Our economic dependence on each other may have decreased, but our emotional dependence has increased. We need that "significant other" so much!

More than ever we need to go back to our spiritual roots and rediscover that which threads its way through human history and unites us across the years with someone as remote as Titus.

Jesus, you are the taproot of our existence. Help us to reaffirm you.

**Find a big old tree. Sit under it, notice its root system, and talk about your differing spiritual roots. Find some common roots.**

# ■ LOVE LETTERS

Philem. 12: "with him goes my heart."

This shortest of all Paul's letters reveals him as the warmest and most loving of friends. His love for the slave Onesimus and his owner Philemon highlights every word.

The letter is a little gospel, preaching the word of forgiveness and reconciliation. The slave master is urged to receive the runaway slave (who may have stolen some money when he left) as a "brother" (v. 16) and to grant him complete pardon. Paul even suggests that Philemon might want to set Onesimus free!

Can you believe that? If you can, then you know what grace is. God never requires penance. Penitence, yes; penance, no. When Onesimus became a brother in the Lord he received everything God had to offer. He didn't have to prove anything.

Oh, to have that kind of ungrudging love! To have the kind of goodness that is not by compulsion but "of your own free will" (v. 14); to be able to say that the one who has wronged you is not only your brother or sister in the Lord but also in the flesh!

Only then can we say, "with him (or her) goes my heart." Grace and love are no longer dogmas that we accept with our intellect, but are woven into the fabric of our emotions. Can we encourage one another, as Paul encouraged Philemon, so that our love for each other will refresh the hearts of the saints?

People do hurt us, God, and we have just grievances. But we pray that our hearts and lives may beat with your grace and love.

**Do you know another couple who once were friends but are now estranged? Would it help to write them a "Philemon letter" and send your very heart?**

# ■ SOMEONE WHO UNDERSTANDS

Heb. 4:14-16: "who was tempted in every way that we are" (v. 15).

*Vive la difference!* is a French saying which applauds the obvious differences between the sexes. Our differences attract and excite us with the possibility of discovery. To be equal need not mean to be identical.

One of the frustrations, however, of being different is revealed in such statements as "Women! Who can understand them?" and "Men! They're all alike!"

In some ways we may never be able to understand persons of the other sex. We have not lived in their skin or walked in their shoes. *She* was never a 12-year-old boy, nor *he* a 12-year-old girl. We were born different and socialized differently.

A picture or a glance that has little effect on one partner may trigger a struggle with temptation in the other. Transcending differences, Jesus Christ is the understanding one who is able to sympathize with our unique weaknesses, because "in every way" he was tempted as we are, yet without sinning.

When we sympathize but just cannot understand the nature of our partner's struggle with temptation, we can honestly say, "I love you and sympathize with you, but I really don't have the understanding I need to be helpful." At that point the best thing we can do is together "approach God's throne, where there is grace" (v. 16). Mercy, grace, and understanding meet us there.

Jesus, give us a heart for each other's struggles with sin.

**Name the differences that you have difficulty understanding in each other.**

# ■ COME TO OUR HOUSE

Heb. 13:2-5: "welcome strangers in your homes"
(v. 2).

We would like to have you come to our home
for dinner next Friday. RSVP." So reads the invitation.
Please come to our home. Dinner. Friday, the end of
a busy week. Sounds like a lot of work. Is hospitality
really a thing of the past?

Couples need to distinguish between *entertaining*
and *hospitality*. Throwing a party *is* work because
there are certain expectations on the part of guests
that advance preparation has been made by the host
couple. The house has been cleaned, hors d'oeuvres
made, and a menu suitable to the occasion planned.
It's an aggressive enterprise to entertain today.

But hospitality is a state of being. To be hospitable
means to be the kind of people who love people.
The house is always ready; if eating happens while
guests are there, they enjoy the fare of the day. A
hospitable couple loves to have people drop by, and
they make their guests feel comfortable and at ease.
Furniture arrangements encourage conversation
and relaxation.

Receiving strangers—the lonely, the outcast, and the
alienated—is basic to Christian hospitality. They are
made to feel wanted, loved, and cared for. The host
and hostess take the lead in seeing that other people
notice them and that they are drawn into the
groupings. That's the kind of home Jesus drops in on.

Lord, bring to our home those who need
hospitality and let them find it.

**Check your home. Is it a hospitable place? What
does the furniture say?**

# ■ HOLD YOUR TONGUE

James 3:5-12: "no one has ever been able to tame the tongue" (v. 8).

Up against males who were bigger than they and upon whom they were dependent for food, shelter, and protection, women developed other ways besides force to manipulate their mates. All a man had to do to get *his* way with a woman was to carry her kicking and screaming into his cave! But one way women learned to get *their* way was by talking. Words became weapons of intimidation or seduction.

The tongue can be used as a strategic weapon. Sin had resulted in men ruling over their wives (Gen. 3:16). Usually defeated in physical contests, women learned what a powerful force the tongue could be!

James does not give much helpful instruction for curbing the tongue's deadly fire. The solution can only be found in Jesus, who tried so hard to break the authority and submission model of relating together. He pointed to the servant role as true greatness, and to children as models. Just before his death he revised his relationship to his disciples and said he was no longer calling them servants but friends (John 15:15).

Friendship and mutual submission take away the need to control each other, through either brute force or verbal abuse. Power games yield to new ways of communicating. Jesus bridles our tongues with a new language of love, and brackish springs pour forth fresh waters of blessing.

Jesus, no human can tame the tongue. But your Spirit can. Bless us, Jesus!

**What effect has "the tongue" had on your relationship?**

# ■ THE LITURGY OF LOVE

James 5:15-16: "confess . . . and pray . . . so that you will be healed" (v. 16).

James tells us that healing of the whole person—body, mind, spirit, and relationships—flows from confessing our sins to one another and praying for one another. Confession opens our lives to the energies of God; prayer channels them into us.

Hold hands and practice this healing therapy with the following litany:

*Husband:* "I confess to you, my wife, that I have sinned against you in these ways. . ." *(Confess the feelings that have blurred your love. Be honest.).* "I am sorry and ask your forgiveness because I don't want anything to stand between us."

*Wife:* "I have heard your confession, my husband, and I forgive you in the name of Jesus and out of my own love for you. I, too, want to confess that I have sinned against you in the following ways . . ." *(Make honest confession of the feelings that have blurred your love.).* "I am sorry and ask your forgiveness because I don't want anything to stand between us."

*Husband:* "I have heard your honest confession, and I forgive you in the name of Jesus and out of my own love for you."

*Together:* "Thank you, Lord, for the healing love which has washed our sins away and made us new people. I thank you for my partner and the love which makes us one. Bless us with total healing of body, mind, and spirit. We praise you for our healed relationship. Amen."

**Repeat the above frequently.**

## ■ SHARE AND SHARE ALIKE

1 Peter 1:3-9: ''the rich blessings that God keeps for his people'' (v. 4).

We married people like to put our properties into "joint tenancy" so that both husband and wife have equal rights of ownership. On the human level it doesn't always work that way. In some states, even if all the necessary legal papers declare that both husband and wife own some property, and even though both have worked equally hard to take care of it, the wife is required to pay inheritance taxes if the husband dies, while he does not have the same obligation if she dies.

God says when it comes to *his* inheritance, it's "share and share alike." No one is left out or gets less. Even the worker who came at the end of the day got the same as those who had worked all day in the vineyard, says the parable (Matt. 20:12). Everyone gets the same imperishable, undefiled, and unfading inheritance from God. No one gets any preferred treatment.

Because we are joint heirs of "God's gift of life" (3:7), both husband and wife deserve equal honor from each other, the kind of respect due to heirs and heiresses. And if one partner happens to have been a Christian longer than the other or knows more Bible verses than the other, that's nice, but it doesn't change the terms of God's will. All who love the Lord Jesus Christ have the same hope, "the salvation of your souls" (v. 9).

Jesus, we thank you for your last will and testament designating us as your joint heirs.

**How do you feel about the fact that you share and share alike?**

# ■ THE MOST PRECIOUS STONE

1 Peter 2:4-9: "the living stone . . . chosen by God as valuable" (v. 4).

If you're a farmer plowing a field and your machinery breaks on surface rocks, you are obviously not going to consider stones as precious objects! But people die in the heat and dust of mines looking for diamonds, and in the search for all manner of precious and semi-precious stones they brave burning deserts and the icy cold of rivers and streams. We wear precious stones to symbolize love, wealth, elegance, and royalty, and the desire to possess them drives people to steal, kill, cheat, lie, and embezzle.

Rocks and stones play starring roles in God's story. Early in the history of Israel Moses sang about God as a rock whose "works are perfect" and warned Israel to obey "the Rock . . . who gave you birth" (Deut. 32:4, 18 NIV). God wrote his law on stone tablets and Joshua planted a great stone at Shechem to remind the people not to be untrue to their God. (Josh. 24:25-26).

Jesus said wise people build their houses on rock, not sand, and foretold the building of his church on the "rock" of his lordship (Matt. 16:13-18).

Claim Jesus as the precious cornerstone of your marriage, the rock of your salvation. Then you have something solid to build upon.

Jesus, precious rock of our salvation, even the stones praise you!

**Go together to find a rock that symbolizes God's precious stone and put it somewhere in the center of your house.**

# ■ POINTERS FROM PETER

1 Peter 3:1-7: "your true inner self" (v. 4).

While the whole idea of a patriarchal society in which a woman was the property of her husband and called him "lord" may be meaningless to egalitarian couples of today, some precepts from Peter, if observed, might prevent much grief in our relationships.

1. If your partner is not a believer, don't try to push him or her into going to church or accepting Christ. Be gentle and show by your behavior what it means to be a Christian. They'll get the idea much better that way.

2. A love based on looking good and dressing up rests on a shaky foundation. Don't build up expectations in your mate that you will always look like Mr. or Mrs. America. Take time instead to find and love the "true inner self" of the other person. If good looks are the basis for your love, anxiety over being seen without the trimmings will create insecurity. And while nudity and seductive clothing are often desirable with one's own mate, immodest appearance in public may arouse sexual interest in others and be a source of anxiety to one's own lover.

3. Be gentle with your wives, men. Any repressive or brutal behavior in Christian husbands must be regarded as a sin of the worst kind. In fact, says Peter, even disrespectful behavior may hinder your prayer life.

Lord, give us reverence for each other's person, both the seen and the unseen.

**How does it make you feel if your lover seems to want to look "sexy" for others? If he or she always looks like a "slob"?**

# ■ JUST A MATTER OF TIME

2 Peter 3:8-13:  "There is no difference in the Lord's sight between one day and a thousand years" (v. 8).

Time is made up of more than sunrises and sunsets, calendars and clocks. Time is both a gift and grace, a sacrament of precious importance. Finite and limited, it has a beginning and an end. We have just so much of it.

From God's perspective our lifetime allotment of time is just a tiny fraction of history. But for us it's *all* of our history, a span of moments, days, and years between birth and death.

For those of us who are lovers of God and each other, every moment is valuable. Because we view time as more than something to be "spent," five minutes together which are rich with loving words and acts can be more rewarding than a month's vacation without that kind of communication.

On the other hand, a day of loveless silence can seem like a thousand years! We can sense what hell must be like, with its absence of love, caring, and all that makes time worthwhile.

Time, says God, will end. A new heaven and a new earth are coming. We'll miss the beautiful love-filled moments we've known here, but we'll feel no grief over the loss of the sin, hatred, and weariness that often makes time hang so heavily on us.

Lord, help us understand the gift of time as a gift of your love.

**Plant some bulbs together. As you wait for their appearance in the spring, what do you learn about God and time and patience?**

# ■ WHAT THE WORLD NEEDS MOST

1 John 4:7-21: "God is love" (v. 8).

Count the number of times the word *love* or a variation of it appears in these 15 verses. In our version we counted 27 instances. Apparently John was in love with love! That figures. Because when you're in love with God you're in love with love, and when you're in love with love you're in love with God.

You just can't help getting the idea that love is what the world needs when you read John's writings. It's the answer to everything, he says. If people love, they'll take care of the physical needs of the poor and oppressed. If they love and are loved, they'll stop being afraid, and all those anxieties born of fear will cease to plague them. Wars and murders and all of the "isms" that hold people down will stop, because we'll love our neighbors. Love is the key to the promised land.

It's too good to be true. Until the prince of this world is put away forever, we've got a constant battle with sin and hatred on our hands. But it's the love of God lived out in the attitudes and behaviors of people that keeps Satan from gaining total control of this world. The fact that people *do* love each other and *do* help one another is the mark of God's presence and the seal of Satan's ultimate destruction.

Only because Jesus showed us how to love is true love possible at all. *He* is what the world needs most.

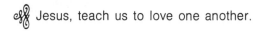 Jesus, teach us to love one another.

**Make a "love chart." Use a calendar, and every day before you go to bed estimate the degree of love shown in your relationship. Mark 1 for the lowest degree, 10 for the highest.**

# ■ JUST ASK ME

1 John 5:14-15:   ''he hears us if we ask him'' (v. 14).

Picture a household scene before Christmas. "If you really loved me you'd know what I want without having to ask me!" Does that sound familiar? Or how about this? "But you never *ask* me to take you out, so how am I going to know that you want me to?"

We're human, and even though we may have been given some hints by our partner, we don't always hear the question behind the innuendos. Sometimes I may choose not to hear the hint because it doesn't fit my wishes or plans.

God knows what we want before we ask, we're told, but the problem is that *we* don't always know. Have we researched what his will is in a particular matter? Have we thought about the consequences of our asking? Does our wish fit the wishes of our mate? Have we discussed it with him or her?

Now if God, with all the unlimited resources at his command, still says "Ask!" why should we expect our mate to know what we want without asking? So many nonverbal messages are misread and result in hurt feelings and alienation. A simple request could have avoided all of the misunderstanding.

Asking also ends the games we play with each other. We are forced into honest expression and responsible response. And with God we lay our faith on the line when we ask. We're saying, "I know you *are*, I believe you *care*, I trust your promise to *listen*, I live in the *hope* of your answer." So *ask*.

God, we're really trying to believe this enormous promise. Help us!

**What direct questions do you avoid asking but hope your spouse will answer out of intuition? How does this affect communication between you?**

# ■ TOUGH LOVE

2 John 8: "Be on your guard, then, so that you will not lose what we have worked for."

Love is a mixture of sweetness and bitterness, tenderness and toughness, but it's all part of the recipe. The beloved child who runs across a highway must be sharply reprimanded if he or she is to be saved. A cardiac arrest requires brutal resuscitation or a terrifying electric shock to restore the heart's function. And a friend who is toying with strange doctrines and demonic delusions must quickly be warned of potential disaster!

When this letter to the "dear lady" was written, about 60 years had passed since the resurrection of Jesus from the dead. All of the apostles except John had been killed. Paul had been beheaded, and Peter crucified upside down. Now false teachers were coming into the church denying that Jesus was the Son of God in the flesh.

"Do not welcome him in your homes," says John, "anyone who wishes him peace becomes his partner in the evil things he does" (vv. 10-11). Not a very open-minded approach, but if the result of listening to false teaching has the same consequence for your life as a child playing on a highway, then why listen?

Do you love one another enough to be tough when necessary? It could be that your love can be measured by the degree to which you want the other one kept in the faith.

Lord, give us the discernment to know false teaching when we see it and a false teacher when we meet one. Above all, help us to follow love.

**Decide together what things you want or do not want to be open-minded about.**

## ■ EYE CONTACT

3 John 14: "we will talk personally."

It has been said that "Marriage is having an eye to catch." Across a crowded room your lover's eyes transmit many messages.

Eyes reveal us, our inner thoughts and feelings. If our mate won't look us in the eye, our anxiety level rises alarmingly. "What's wrong? What have I done? What's being hidden?" When we've lived with someone for any time at all it doesn't take long to know what the eyes are saying.

We learn to read each other's signs, and we become good senders and decoders of nonverbal interpersonal messages. The sudden smile, a rush of tears to the eyes, a trembling chin and quivering lips communicate many meanings.

John had something to say to Gaius that could not be adequately communicated in writing. He had to "talk personally." Gaius' eyes had to tell John their reactions, and Gaius had to know that the words said were out of John's love for him and not out of anger or a spirit of judgment.

One wrong word or misunderstood phrase in a written message takes a long time to explain. If it's more comfortable for you to communicate in writing, be sure to be face to face when you read each other's messages. Then your eyes will give life and spirit to your words and reveal the depth of your love.

Jesus, let our eye messages to each other be lovingly sent and lovingly received.

**Check to see if you're decoding your lover's eye messages accurately.**

# ■ NET UNDER THE SWAYING BRIDGE

Jude 24-25: "To him who is able to keep you from falling" (v. 24).

Reading Jude is like walking across a chasm on a swaying footbridge. Just when you think you've almost made it to the other side you see a bear starting down the path toward you.

Being a Christian is like that, says Jude. Just when you are convinced that your salvation has been received, you find yourself having to contend for the faith! Along the path are heretics, fallen angels, the devil, and scoffers. In descriptive language Jude calls these deceivers:

"dirty spots in your fellowship meals. . . .

"clouds carried along by the wind, but bringing no rain. . . .

"trees that . . . are completely dead. . . .

"wild waves of the sea, with their shameful deeds showing up like foam. . . .

"wandering stars, for whom God has reserved a place forever in the deepest darkness" (vv. 12-13).

In other words, watch out!

But under the swaying footbridge between new birth and new life God has strung a net. In one of the most comforting of all benedictions, Jude writes about God's keeping power. He won't let you fall. You can trust him to "bring you faultless and joyful before his glorious presence" (v. 24).

God is exactly what he has promised: our Savior through Jesus Christ. He is the net into which we fall, the arm to prevent our injury. To him be honor and glory, dominion and power!

Savior God, we trust you to keep us from betraying you and each other.

**Memorize this Bible passage.**

# ■ HANG IN THERE

Revelation 2-3:  "To those who win the victory . . ."
(2:7, 11, 17, 26-28; 3:5, 12, 21).

Although a blessing is promised to all who read the Revelation to John (1:3), much of the book defies accurate interpretation. However, there's no mistaking the messages to the seven churches in chapters 2 and 3.

To some a word of judgment and warning was given; to others comfort and encouragement. To all a word of exhortation brought hope and the will to carry on: "Hang in there! To the one who conquers the rewards are worth the struggle!"

Christians in John's day were being thrown to the lions, killed by gladiators in the Roman coliseum, and covered with pitch and burned as torches to light the Appian Way. John himself was in exile on the island of Patmos, off the west coast of Asia Minor.

Christians could have escaped this persecution by performing one simple act: offering sacrifices before a statue of the Roman emperor. There were many who chose this alternative. But some could not deny that Jesus was Lord. How could they engage in such pagan idolatry? Many of these faithful believers suffered arrest, confiscation of their possessions, and death.

Do the struggles of your life make you wonder if being a Christian is worth the effort? Are you tempted to deny Christ by yielding to something you know is against his will but which would gratify your desires? Can you hang in there even when others tell you how stupid it is to deny yourself and to bear your cross with Jesus?

Lord God Almighty, Alpha and Omega, help us make it to the end.

**List the rewards promised in the seven letters to those who conquer.**

# ■ HALLELUJAH CHORUS

Rev. 7:9-12: "Salvation comes from our God" (v. 10).

Marriage is God's way of teaching us to say "we" instead of "I" and "our" instead of "my." That may be its most important but most difficult lesson.

From the day I was born the world centered about *me*. My wishes came first; my wants were expressed in no uncertain terms. I demanded instant gratification. The bottle or breast had to be available when I wanted food. Somebody had to be around to pick me up when I needed loving, or I would yell until they came running!

My marriage succeeds to the degree that I am able to incorporate the needs of my lover with my own needs. *Our* needs must have priority. If that happens, we're on our way to Christian maturity. From *my* world I begin to care about *our* world. The "Our Father" of the Lord's Prayer begins to shape the expression of our faith.

Slowly we are getting ready for the world to come. In heaven *our* God is praised and honored. Every nation, tribe, and language is represented in its neighborhoods. Imagine the "Hallelujah Chorus" sung in thousands of different tongues by a completely integrated choir! No mention of 144,000 here; this chorus is a great multitude which no one can count! The white robes come in all sizes to cover children as well as women and men of every skin hue and facial feature imaginable!

Lamb of God, we can't wait!

**Every time you say "I" instead of "we" when talking about your common life, put a quarter in a box and give it to your church mission program.**

# ■ THE INTIMACY OF SILENCE

Rev. 8:1-6: "there was silence in heaven for about half an hour" (v. 1).

Silence. What's happening when words stop? In the Revelation to John it marked the beginning of cataclysmic events. It was the quiet before the storm, the breathless moment of expectation. Pregnant with meaning, silence is often the forerunner of heavy conversation.

But silence may also be communication in the deepest sense. When we are one flesh words may not always be needed. They are superfluous when identification with the other is complete.

We have come beyond that awful fear of our adolescent dating, "What will we talk about?" We do not need to fill every moment with chatter. In those days if we didn't have something to say we felt naked and embarrassed, awkward and terrified.

Silence sometimes provides couples a barrier against saying too much. Breaking it would open the floodgates to words that might end in tears or blows. Topics that usually lead to arguments can be avoided through silence. When silence is comfortable we can experience an intimacy that words can never express.

Being still and quiet in the presence of God prepares us for what may previously have been "sealed" information. Silence is a prerequisite for God's deepest revelations.

Lord, we hear you in the silence. Give us quietness of spirit.

**Sit facing each other. Express your feelings for your lover nonverbally.**

# ■ THE LAST WEDDING

Rev. 21:4: "He will wipe away all tears from their eyes."

The Bible begins and ends with a wedding. The first wedding ended with disobedience and tears of sin and alienation from God. The last wedding brings reunion with the Lord and tears of joy and reconciliation.

Why do people cry at weddings? If members of the family don't cry, then certainly someone in the audience will have moist eyes. What brings the tears? Are they wrung from the memory of a broken relationship or the bitter residue of unrequited love? Maybe a parent is simply having a hard time letting a child go. Or tears may well up out of the joyful recognition of two loving people entering into high human happiness.

John, the "beloved disciple," was caught up in the ultimate marriage-to-be. All of us who are pledged to Jesus will consummate our engagement as a bride adorned for her husband. No celebration we have known can touch the elegance and pathos of this final union with our Lord.

All tears that have wet your cheeks will be wiped away as God removes forever all cause for them. Life will have the last laugh on death as the one who sits on the throne says, "And now I make all things new!" (21:5). The new Jerusalem is our ultimate destiny, and we look forward to meeting our beloved Lord there with as much eagerness as any bride and groom embarking on their honeymoon journey.

Lord, sometimes the wonder of our love makes us weep for joy.

**When did you last feel so full of love that you cried?**

# ■ SHALOM, LORD JESUS!

Rev. 22:16-21: " 'I am coming soon!' So be it.
Come, Lord Jesus" (v. 20).

Life moves on so fast. One day it's your wedding
day, then a moment later your fifth anniversary. In a
twinkling of time, it's the tenth, the twenty-fifth,
the fiftieth. . . .

You look back on the years, the good ones and the
tough ones. Ah, that was the year we went to Europe.
That was great! And that was the year I broke my
leg skiing. It was tough being laid up all that time.
And then there was that year we almost got a divorce.
Didn't think we'd make it, but by the grace of God
and a lot of help from our friends. . . .

For some of you just starting out, that all seems a
long way off. And of course it is. It's a lifetime. How
does it happen? By living one day at a time. Your
morning prayer can be, "Lord, help us to live lovingly
just this one day." Your evening prayer can be, "Lord,
thank you for helping us live lovingly today. Now we
ask your blessing on our night and thank you for
the privilege of being together."

The days grow into weeks, months, years, and
anniversaries. Deeper love, shining moments, tender
moments. And through it all you learn to trust in Jesus
and depend on the promises of God. You come full
circle. Past, present, and future are all one piece—
timeless like the presence of God, who is the beginning
and the end.

So *shalom*, beloved! And *shalom*, Lord Jesus! Amen.

Jesus, you have been our bright morning and
evening star. We love you.

**Shalom is both hello and good-bye, and everything
good. What is your *shalom* wish for your lover today?**

# BIBLE READINGS SERIES

*Bible Readings for Women*
    Lyn Klug
*Bible Readings for Men*
    Steve Swanson
*Bible Readings for Parents*
    Ron and Lyn Klug
*Bible Readings for Couples*
    Margaret and Erling Wold
*Bible Readings for Singles*
    Ruth Stenerson
*Bible Readings for Families*
    Mildred and Luverne Tengbom
*Bible Readings for Teenagers*
    Charles S. Mueller
*Bible Readings for Mothers*
    Mildred Tengbom
*Bible Readings for Teachers*
    Ruth Stenerson
*Bible Readings for Students*
    Ruth Stenerson
*Bible Readings for the Retired*
    Leslie F. Brandt
*Bible Readings for Church Workers*
    Harry N. Huxhold
*Bible Readings for Office Workers*
    Lou Ann Good
*Bible Readings for Growing Christians*
    Kevin E. Ruffcorn
*Bible Readings for Caregivers*
    Betty Groth Syverson
*Bible Readings for Troubled Times*
    Leslie F. Brandt
*Bible Readings for Farm Living*
    Frederick Baltz
*Bible Readings on Prayer*
    Ron Klug
*Bible Readings on Hope*
    Roger C. Palms
*Bible Readings on God's Creation*
    Denise J. Williamson